JUDAISM
AND THE
WORLD'S RELIGIONS

JUDAISM
AND THE
WORLD'S RELIGIONS

David Bamberger

BEHRMAN HOUSE, INC., PUBLISHERS
SPRINGFIELD, NEW JERSEY

To the memory of my father
Rabbi Bernard J. Bamberger
who told me the story about the white light
(see Chapter 2)

PROJECT EDITOR: Nicolas D. Mandelkern
BOOK DESIGNER: Gilda Hannah
MAP ARTIST: Allen Aldridge

Published by Behrman House, Inc.
11 Edison Place, Springfield, New Jersey 07081
Manufactured in the United States of America

ISBN 0-87441-461-X

Library of Congress Cataloging-in-Publication Data

Bamberger, David.
  Judaism and the world's religions.

  1. Judaism—Relations. 2. Religions. I. Title.
BM534.B36 1987   296.3'872   87-18691

Contents

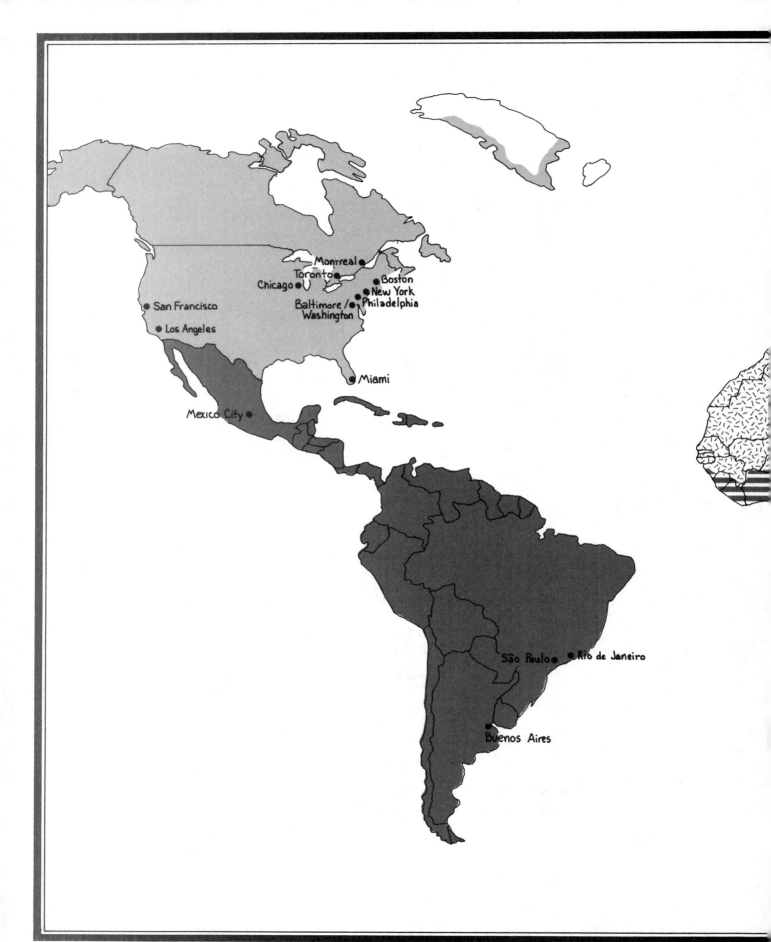

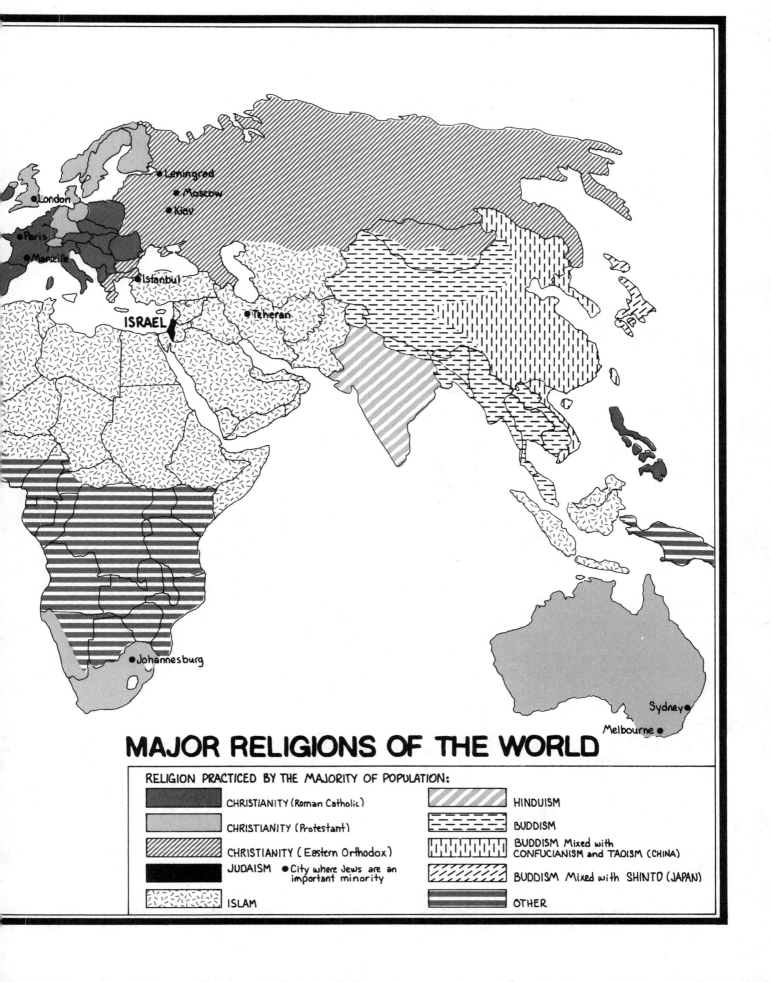

MAJOR RELIGIONS OF THE WORLD

RELIGION PRACTICED BY THE MAJORITY OF POPULATION:

CHRISTIANITY (Roman Catholic)

CHRISTIANITY (Protestant)

CHRISTIANITY (Eastern Orthodox)

JUDAISM • City where Jews are an important minority

ISLAM

HINDUISM

BUDDISM

BUDDISM Mixed with CONFUCIANISM and TAOISM (CHINA)

BUDDISM Mixed with SHINTO (JAPAN)

OTHER

PART ONE
BEGINNING TO EXPLORE

1 DECIDING WHAT MATTERS

Is Judaism special?

Does it matter if you are a Jew?

As a Jew, you are a member of a tiny minority group, one which has often faced persecution simply for claiming the right to exist. Fortunately, Jews in America are not threatened in this way—but being Jewish still makes us different. We celebrate different holidays. We attend different religious schools. We have a different kind of concern for the State of Israel.

Is it worth it?

Is it worth the time, the effort, and perhaps the risk, of being part of the Jewish people?

How Great a Difference?

On the simplest level, the differences we are talking about may simply be a matter of preferring our customs to those of other religions. The special foods and activities of the Passover Seder may seem more appealing than the Easter celebrations which take place about the same time. Eight nights of Ḥanukkah may seem a more fun celebration than the single day of Christmas.

When the Bible speaks of our being different, however, it is talking about something else. It is dealing with the whole universe. The Torah states that God has chosen us to be God's special people. In it, God tells us:

> If you will obey me faithfully, you shall be My treasured possession among all the peoples of the earth. All the earth is Mine, but you shall be a kingdom of priests and a holy nation. [Exodus 19:5–6]

Other Nations

If we are the chosen people, how does God view other nations?

This question was debated about 2,000 years ago, by some of our greatest scholars and teachers. The Talmud reports a discussion among them as to what would become of non-Jews after their death. If they were not of God's chosen people, could they share the same fate as Jews?

The decision was that it would be unjust for God to punish righteous people simply because they were not Jewish. God is a just God. Therefore, says the Talmud:

The righteous of all nations will have a share in the world-to-come. [*Talmud, Sanhedrin 8b*]

Sometimes we believe two things that seem at first to contradict each other. Thomas Jefferson (left), wrote in the Declaration of Independence that "all men are created equal." But we know that people are very different in looks, personalities, and skills. Why are *both* things true?

Resolving an Apparent Contradiction

The two quotations seem to contradict each other. On the one hand, Jews are chosen to be God's special people. On the other hand, the righteous of all nations are equally welcome in "the world-to-come."

The resolution is not difficult to find. The first quotation does not suggest that Jews are superior in any way to other groups. It says only that God has decided to make us a chosen people—*if* we obey God's commandments.

And the Bible does not suggest that our reward will be riches, or power, or even a special place "in the world-to-come." It says simply that our reward will be to become "a holy nation." The full meaning of this idea is made clear in the Book of Isaiah:

I the Lord have called you in righteousness
To be a light to the nations of the world.
[*Isaiah 42:6*]

In other words, God has chosen the Jewish people to be *teachers*. God has given us the job of learning right and wrong, good and evil, and then teaching these things to the other nations of the world.

What to Teach?

But what are we supposed to teach? What does Judaism say that is *so* special that we should tell others about it?

Or, to get back to our first question: is Judaism really special?

To answer that question, we will have to find out what Judaism teaches, and how it differs from other great religions. We will need to learn the key ideas of some of the most important people who ever lived.

And in doing so, we will find out a great deal about ourselves.

WHY THE JEWS?

Why did God give the Torah to the Jews? Because the Jews were so much better than other people?

No. According to our rabbis, God offered the Torah to every nation. God wanted all people to enjoy it, learn from it, and live by it.

But nation after nation refused to accept the Torah. One examined it and found, "You shall not murder." "This is not for us," they said. "We are soldiers and fighters. We do not want that law."

Another nation saw the commandment, "You shall not steal." "This is not for us," they said. "We have wealthy neighbors. We make a good living by taking whatever we need."

So it went. Every nation refused God's teaching. At last God came to the people of Israel. They too looked at the laws. They found instructions like, "You shall love your neighbor as yourself."

And the people of Israel said, "All that the Lord has spoken we will do and we will obey." [*Exodus 24:7*]

2 MOTOR IDEAS

An engine needs fuel. It may run on gasoline, or steam, or electricity. Without some kind of fuel, the motor will not run.

Nations, too, need "fuel" to keep them running. They need natural resources, government, roads, and so on. Yet to keep a nation's "motor" going—the motor which keeps a nation moving, creating, and developing—another kind of "fuel" is needed.

That kind of fuel is provided by ideas.

These *motor ideas* can be some of the most powerful forces on earth.

Just as a motor can take a huge rocket and thrust it through the sky at great speeds, a motor idea can move a society to powerful activity.

Motor Ideas: Hitler

One example of "motor ideas" are those that Adolf Hitler taught the German people. According to Hitler, the Germans were a superior race, destined to rule the world; and the Jews were less than human—villains who wanted to destroy Germany. Therefore, they should be killed.

These ideas so excited the Germans that they made Hitler the ruler of Germany. He sent out armies which conquered most of Europe and North Africa before they were finally defeated. At the same time, Hitler's Germany murdered six million Jews.

Motor Ideas: Democracy

Nations like the United States, England, and Israel are driven by totally different motor ideas. We believe that every nation has the right to live in freedom, that no nation should rule another, and that no person should be murdered because of beliefs.

These motor ideas led England, America, and other countries to fight against Hitler in the Second World War. This clash of motor ideas lasted for six years. During that time, fifteen million soldiers and at least fifteen million civilians died.

Are ideas really all that important? As the Second World War proved, motor ideas can be very powerful forces indeed.

One of Judaism's most powerful motor ideas can be found in the Torah: "You shall love your neighbor as yourself." Judaism's motor ideas led the world's Jews to help their fellow Jews escape from starvation and oppression in Ethiopia and start new lives in Israel.

Huge crowds line the route of a religious festival in Japan. Throughout the world, billions of people practice hundreds of different religions. Although Judaism is one of the world's most significant religions, Jews make up less than one-half of one percent of the world's total population.

Motor Ideas: Religion

Many of the world's most powerful and important motor ideas have come from the world's great religions.

Religions have brought valuable ideas to the world. They have given meaning to the lives of their followers, and often inspired these men and women to behave in a moral way. As we have seen, Judaism recognizes this: "The righteous of all nations will have a share in the world to come."

Yet if people say, "We are Jews," they should be saying, "We remain Jews because we think there is something truly special about *our* religion."

Translating this into the terms we have been using, a person who says "I am a Jew" should also be saying: "The motor ideas and ideals of Judaism are the most valuable developed by any religion in the world."

What a Thing to Say!

That is really quite a thing to say. The most valuable ideas of *any* religion in the world!

We don't like to think in those terms. We deeply believe that all people should have the right to their own beliefs, and we would rather not say that the ideas of our non-Jewish friends just aren't as valuable as ours.

Yet if we felt their ideas were *more* valuable than ours, we would naturally adopt them. Even if we thought their ideas were equal in value to ours, we might be tempted to simplify things by blending in with the majority.

No—when you say, "I am a Jew," you are implying that there is something particularly worthwhile about Judaism which is worth preserving. You may not have thought much about other religions, or know much about them, but at least you are accepting what your parents and teachers are implying when they say, "I am a Jew."

This book is designed to help you make those decisions for yourself. It will introduce you to the basic motor ideas of the world's most important religions. You will see how very different they are, and what a unique place Judaism has in the history of human thought. You will be happier and prouder than ever to be identified with the ideas and ideals of Judaism.

A Certain Discomfort

And yet you may still be uncomfortable.

You know that billions of people in the world are not Jewish. Most of them consider their religion to be the best. How can we say that our religion is particularly right without saying that the rest of the world is particularly wrong?

Seeing the Light

A great rabbi answered that question with the following story:

Once there was a very unusual building. It had five sides, and in every side there was a glass window. At the center of the building was a bright light.

It was announced that the world's greatest prize would go to that person who could describe, exactly, the color of the light.

Those who looked through one window announced, "The light is red." From another window came a group announcing, "There is almost no light, yet we found it. It is a very, very dark blue." "Green," said another. "Violet." "A very pale yellow."

No one received the prize.

The Answer

Perhaps you have realized the right answer. The light was perfectly white—but each person was seeing it through colored glass.

Each answer was partly correct. White light is actually a mixture of many colors—the ones we see when the light separates to form a rainbow. But this doesn't mean that each group was equally right. The group that saw the light as pale yellow was almost right. The group at the very dark blue glass that saw almost nothing was almost completely wrong.

Judaism teaches that there is a light at the center of the world. That light is God. We realize that no one can understand God perfectly. We all seem to be looking from a distance, through a different-colored window.

We know that all peoples can see part of God's light, through one "window" or another.

Yet, having listened carefully to the ideas of all the world's religions, we still believe that the clearest glass through which to see God's light is the window of Judaism.

All over the world people are trying to see God. But we all seem to be looking through different windows.

Summary

Every nation is driven by different key beliefs, which can be called "motor ideas." These ideas can be extraordinarily powerful. A clash of ideas generated the Second World War. Religions have been the source of many powerful "motor ideas." Jews recognize that many religions have generated important and useful concepts. By being Jewish, however, we state that we see the ideas and ideals of Judaism as being the most valuable motor ideas developed by any religion in the world.

3 WORSHIPPING MANY GODS

Many animals live in ways that are similar to humans.

Gorillas show tender care for their children. Dolphins talk to each other. Birds may live together in colonies. Some ants organize as an effective army.

But only humans have learned to worship God. Every human society has its religion. Even the most primitive tribes have some form of worship.

This worship usually involves some sort of statue showing an image of a god or spirit. It might be made of stone, or metal, or glass, or wood. It might be a giant human being, or an animal, or a fantastic monster. It might be very small or very large. Such images of primitive gods are known as *idols*.

Idol Worship Solves a Problem

Ancient societies worshipped many idols of many gods. One nation had so many idols that the people simply did not have time to worship them all. This worried the people. They feared that if the idols did not receive enough attention, the gods might become angry and punish the people with disasters.

They found a clever solution. If a statue could be a god, then a statue could also be a worshipper! They made statues of worshippers, and placed them before statues of gods. Since "someone" was always "praying" to each idol, the people felt confident that the gods would not be angry.

This ingenious experiment did not last very long. The empires collapsed, the idols crumbled. The names of these ancient gods are remembered only by scholars.

Egypt of the Pharaohs

One of the most impressive religions of ancient times was in Egypt. Since the land was rich and powerful, magnificent monuments could be built to the gods. Among the gods to be

Termites can build huge forts. These buildings may stand more than twenty feet high and contain ten tons of dried mud. They even have special tunnels to carry air and keep the fort cool. But human beings are the only animals to know there is a God, and to create buildings in God's honor.

honored were the kings, known as *pharaohs*, who were believed to be the actual children of gods born to rule the earth. The early *pharaohs* were honored with gigantic tombs, such as the great pyramids. The largest of these was built about 4,600 years ago, and is still the largest stone building in the world. It contains over 2,000,000 blocks of stone, most weighing two-and-a-half tons. The base of the pyramid would cover more than eleven football fields! Yet the mammoth structure was put together with amazing accuracy. Its opposite corners are within half an inch of being perfectly level.

In Life and Death

Pharaohs were not the only Egyptian gods; there were many more. Most of them were thought of as animals, or often animals combined with the body of a human. Hawks, dogs, cats, baboons, and crocodiles all became idols that were worshipped.

The gods were thought to control every activity of daily life. Even more important to the Egyptians, the gods controlled life after death. The Egyptians believed that death opened to them another world where they could continue to enjoy life as they had on earth.

It was a long trip to the next life—and the traveler had to be prepared. First, he had to have a body! So the Egyptians discovered the way to make *mummies* to preserve the dead body

This stone idol, found in northern Syria, was an object of worship over 3,000 years ago.

The finest craftsmen of ancient Egypt used gold and other precious metals to create a case for the mummy of their king. By protecting his corpse, they felt they guaranteed him eternal life.

Ancient Egyptians thought of one of their gods as a friendly cat. Other ancient peoples imagined their gods in different ways. In parts of South America, for example, god was seen as a fierce jaguar. Does this difference remind you of the story of people seeing God's light while looking through different windows?

and keep it from decaying. Then they buried the mummy with containers of food, clothing, chariots, weapons—everything needed to enjoy an endless life after death.

In the New World

The gods of Egypt were thought to be quite friendly. The gods who ruled the tribes of Central and South America were not. The Aztec Indians, for example, were, like the Egyptians, a very cultured people. They also had clever architects, and built huge pyramids. But on the top of each pyramid they built an altar where they offered human sacrifices. They would take a victim and, while he was still alive, cut out his heart as an offering to their gods. The flowing blood was thought to supply the sun god with nourishment.

The Worship of Many Gods: Polytheism

Every ancient society worshipped many gods. Whether friendly or unfriendly, human or animal-shaped, ordinary or monstrous, there were always many gods to be served.

The worship of many gods is known as *polytheism*. (This word is made up of two Greek terms: *poly*—"many," and *theos*—"god.")

Polytheism is very different from what we think of as religion, but it is easy to understand why ancient peoples favored it. Perhaps a man saw the sun and the power of its rays. He prayed for good weather. The sun did shine and he was grateful. He began to worship the sun.

A woman was thirsty. She prayed for rain, and it came. She decided to bring gifts regularly to the rain god.

A child was lost at night, but the moon lit the way home. The moon must be a kindly god! And so on. . .

The Problem With Polytheism

The problem with polytheism is that it sees each force of nature as separate and independent. There is no plan in the universe. What happens to us is imagined to reflect the moods of the gods—or of whatever god happens to be in control at a particular time and place. A short distance away, another god might rule.

Polytheism can tell us very little about what is truly right and wrong. Whatever you want to do will have some god or other who approves of it. The ancient Greeks, for example, had major gods who did extraordinarily wicked things. They even had gods assigned to protect thieves and drunks!

Gods had different tastes. Worship of one god might have to be very different from the worship of another. Some were said to be jealous of each other, so in serving one god you had to be sure not to insult a powerful rival.

It was a tricky thing to keep all these gods happy!

Sacrifices

Usually this was done by giving presents to the gods. These were often food items which could be burned so that the pleasing smell of the food would rise to gods' heavenly homes. An offering given in this way is called a *sacrifice*.

Some gods were said to demand very special kinds of sacrifices. In the land of Israel, before the Jewish people existed, there were tribes called *Canaanites*. The Canaanites had many gods, but one they thought was especially powerful was named Moloch. His priests said that Moloch required the sacrifice of children.

To keep the god Moloch content, live babies—usually firstborn males—were burned to death inside flaming idols.

Polytheism teaches us little about right and wrong. The ancient Aztecs, as this sixteenth-century drawing shows, believed in sacrificing humans to their sun-god, and even tore out the victim's living heart.

Some polytheistic cultures worship their ancestors as gods. This wooden statue, from the Congo basin of central Africa, represents a female ancestor of the Kuba people.

Motor Ideas: Polytheism

The motor ideas of polytheism, therefore, seem very peculiar to us. They are:

- The world is organized by chance. There is no plan or order in the universe.

- There is no single system of right and wrong. Whatever you want to do will find the approval of one god or another.

- The gods rule according to their own moods.

- There is no limit to what must be done to keep each of the gods happy, even if this requires the sacrifice of little children.

This is what all the world believed. One man was to change it. His name was Abraham.

Summary

Every human society has had a religion. In ancient times, religions used idols in the worship of many gods, a practice known as *polytheism*. The problem with polytheism is that each god has his own tastes and moods, so there is no single system of right and wrong. The worshipper must decide how to keep each god happy without making other gods angry. Sacrifices—in some cases, child sacrifices—were used to provide gifts to the gods.

HONORING ANCIENT GODS

Although we often think of idol-worshippers as "primitive," some polytheistic cultures have created works which still inspire amazement.

A pharaoh of ancient Egypt built this huge monument to honor himself. Each of the four statues of the king was originally sixty-seven feet high, and was carved out of a cliff facing the Nile River. Many scholars believe that he was the pharaoh who made slaves out of the Hebrew people, and that he used them on huge building projects like this one.

Terrible storms, fierce heat, and wild animals—all of these are found in the rain forest of Guatemala. Yet there the Mayan Indians built a city, crowned by this 145-foot Temple of the Giant Jaguar.

No one knows the exact purpose of Stonehenge, this structure of huge stones in southern England. Some people have suggested that it could have been used to record the position of the sun, moon and stars, and to allow the ancient Britons to know when eclipses would take place. Whatever the purpose, it is amazing that it could be built at all. The stones had to be hauled 20 miles or more—and they weigh as much as 100,000 pounds.

Beautiful things do not need to be huge. The Hebrews had just come from wandering in the desert when the Chinese were making beautiful artwork in bronze. The ancient Chinese worshipped their ancestors. These vessels were used in those ceremonies.

In the ancient Middle East, steps leading to the top of a high tower symbolized the link between humans and gods. These are the remains of such a tower in Iran. The most famous, a 300-foot tower in Babylon, has disappeared, but it is remembered in the Torah where "Babylon" is shortened to "Babel." The *Tower of Babel* is recalled as an attempt of humans to build until they could actually reach to heaven.

The ancient Greeks believed that beautiful things expressed eternal values. Their temple to the goddess of wisdom, Athena, is thought to have been one of the most beautiful buildings in the ancient world. Many modern structures, from banks to government buildings, have imitated its simple but elegant design.

PART TWO
JUDAISM

4 One God of the World

Abraham was just a shepherd. He had no throne, no chariots, no palace. He built no monuments. He was not buried with gold or jewels.

We call Abraham "the first Jew," but in his day the word "Jew" did not exist. (It comes from the name of his great-grandson, Judah. The people of Abraham were called "Hebrews.") The only information on him comes from stories in the Torah. The story of his life is told in just a few chapters.

Yet Abraham changed the history of the world.

A Brief Tale

The key story about Abraham takes only seven of the Bible's verses. God speaks to Abraham, telling him to leave his native land and move to the land of Canaan. God gives Abraham a promise:

> "I will make you a great nation,
> And I will bless you.
> All the families of the earth
> Shall bless themselves by you."
> [Genesis 12:2–3]

As for the land of Canaan, God said:

> "I will give this land to your descendants."
> [Genesis 12:7]

The Results

This is a brief tale in which an invisible God makes grand promises to a wandering shepherd. Such a story would not be worth noticing, except:

- Today the descendants of Abraham, the Jews, are one of the important peoples of the world.

- Today about half the people on earth practice religions which trace their history back to Abraham.

- Today Jews have a state of their own, the State of Israel, in what was once the land of Canaan.

The promises made to Abraham some 4,000 years ago have come true.

One God

A short story in the Bible helped inspire the birth of the State of Israel! That would be enough to make the story significant, but there is an idea of even greater importance that lies behind the story. The idea is not stated directly. Yet in Abraham's day, it was revolutionary.

It is the idea that there is only *one* God.

God speaks to Abraham—and Abraham listens. He doesn't ask for God's name. He doesn't worry if a more powerful god may say something else. He doesn't wonder, what this god has to do with the land of Canaan even though the story takes place many hundreds of miles away.

No. For Abraham there is one God. It is the God who can make promises to children who are not yet born. It is the God

This shepherd in the Negev desert, in the south of Israel, lives much the same way Abraham lived 4,000 years ago. But Abraham's discovery of the one God changed the history of the world.

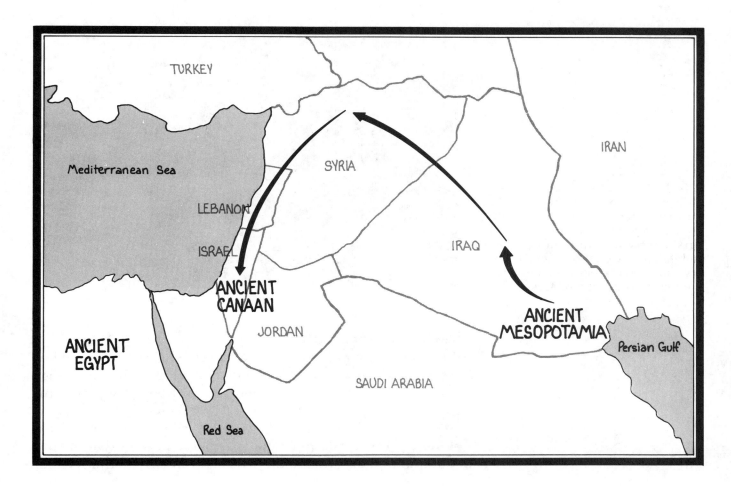

who controls his native land, and the land of Canaan as well. It is the one God of the world.

Motor Ideas: Monotheism

Belief in one God is called *monotheism*. Monotheism is one of the great motor ideas of history. As monotheism was developed in Judaism, it taught ideas exactly opposite to polytheism.

The motor ideas of Judaism are:

- The one God has one plan for the universe. The world is not organized by chance (as polytheism), but according to God's design.

- There is one standard of right and wrong. You cannot do whatever you like, thinking some god or other will approve. The one God has one set of rules of what is *really* right and *really* wrong.

- One of the standards concerns human life. The God who created us believes that life is to be preserved, protected, and developed.

God's commands sent Abraham on a journey of over 1,000 miles from his prosperous homeland to the poor land of Canaan. This land, promised to him and his descendants, is today the State of Israel.

It is dangerous for Russian Jews to observe their religion, but still they join together to celebrate Simhat Torah—rejoicing in the Torah. In this rare and unusual picture smuggled out of the Soviet Union, Jews are seen celebrating outside of the main synagogue of Moscow.

Learning God's Rules

If there is one set of rules for the universe, where are we to find them? How are we to learn God's standard of right and wrong?

To begin with, we study the Bible. The part of the Bible which contains the most basic of God's laws is the most sacred book of Judaism, the *Torah* (also called "The Five Books of Moses."). The rules it contains are so important that, though containing many stories, the whole Torah is sometimes called *The Law*.

Its most famous rules are the Ten Commandments. We are told to observe the Sabbath, to honor our parents, to turn away from murder and theft and falsehood. But before we would be ready to obey an order, we want to know who is giving it! So the Ten Commandments begin with a reminder that the source of these laws is the *one* God, the God who saved our people from slavery:

> I am the Lord your God, who brought you out of the land of Egypt, out of the house of slavery. You will have no other God. [*Exodus 20:2–3*]

The Chosen People

The First Commandment reminds us of the key event in early Jewish history, the moment the people of Israel received the Law at Mount Sinai. God's Torah became the special possession of the Jews. The Jews became the special possession of God.

One thing the Jews could have done would have been to say, "We have God on our side—let's conquer the world." Instead, Judaism developed the idea that the highest goal of our people was to help *God's teaching* to conquer the world. The idea of becoming God's chosen people was taken—not as an excuse to make ourselves richer—but as a challenge to make the *world* better.

Each Person Has Value

We say "the world"—but for which people in the world? Judaism answered with another revolutionary idea: We must work to make it better for *all* humanity. *Every* human being has value.

When Judaism began, many religions demanded human sacrifices. Judaism values human life so much that it eliminated such bloody forms of worship. But that is not all. It rarely permits criminals to be executed, even for crimes like murder.

Some religions, as we shall see, divide humanity into different groups, so that people of one group must not even touch people of another. Other religions have set their leaders apart from the rest of humanity by special laws, sometimes crediting them with magical powers.

Judaism has insisted on equality. Jews look to the very first chapters of the Torah, and find one man and one woman—the parents of all humanity.

And so our rabbis, though they are respected for their special learning, are not thought of as having superhuman powers. Any Jew can pray to God or lead services in the synagogue.

Jews believe that all are equal before God. At the age of 13, a boy becomes Bar Mitzvah—entitled to the same rights and subject to the same laws as all adult Jews. The Rabbi is respected for learning and leadership, but is not thought of as having special powers or a closer connection to God.

Election day in an Arab district of Israel. The ballot box is marked with Hebrew words stating "Elections for Parliament." The Jewish belief in equality has led to the creation of the only democracy in the Middle East.

As early as the age of thirteen, a Jewish child earns the right to read in public from the Torah.

We are all equal, says Judaism, in the sight of God. We are all equally responsible for living good lives in accordance with God's commands.

It is not only in setting guidelines for each individual that monotheism has been a powerful motor idea. Thousands of years before the American Declaration of Independence, Judaism believed that "all men are created equal." Today the Jewish State, Israel, is the only country in the Middle East with a democratic government based on this view.

Summary

The Bible brought to the world monotheism—the belief in one God. This became one of the great motor ideas in world history. It meant there was one plan for the universe, and one set of rules to determine right and wrong. In Judaism, this led to a belief in the value of all human beings, and the value of human life. From the story of Abraham we also learn that God has chosen our people to have a home in the land of Israel, and to bring God's message to the rest of the world.

5 LOOKING AT THE WORLD

Imagine a glass filled halfway with lemonade. How would you describe it? Is the glass half full or half empty?

Either answer is correct, of course. But they are also quite different.

The Bright Side

To say the glass is half *full* is to look at the bright side of things. It is to speak about the part of the glass which has lemonade—the good side. To say it is half full suggests that, perhaps, someone will bring some more water and lemons, and it will soon be totally full.

A person who looks at the bright side of things is called an *optimist.*

The Dark Side

To say the glass is half *empty* is to look at the dark side of things. It is to speak about the part of the glass which has nothing—the bad side. To say it is half empty suggests that someone is about to finish the rest of it, and that soon it will be totally empty.

A person who looks at the dark side of things is called a *pessimist.*

Judaism—the Religion of Optimism

Judaism is distinctive in being a religion which takes an optimistic view of the world. The very first paragraph in the first chapter of the Torah tells that God created light, and that God saw how good the light was. And, after the last day of creation and the creation of man and woman, the Bible tells us:

God saw all that He had made, and found it very good.

[*Genesis 1:31*]

Wedding guests dance around the bride at an Orthodox Jewish wedding. They will soon toast the newlyweds with the traditional expression of Jewish hope: *l'chaim*—"to life!"

Enjoying the World

We know this story so well that it seems obvious to us. But its meaning, as understood by the Jewish people, is far from obvious.

Jews firmly believe that the world God created for us is good. We believe that God meant us to enjoy the many wonderful things given us. We are to enjoy beauty. We are to enjoy delicious foods. We are to enjoy our bodies. We are to enjoy the opportunities the world gives us for friendship, for family, for homes filled with love.

Since we believe all humans are equal before God, we expect our religious leaders to enjoy life. Our rabbis enjoy the pleasures of home and family, just as do other Jews.

No Jewish Hermits

This view is very different from many other religions, which see the world as evil. The beauties of the world are, in this view, just bait in a trap. The more we enjoy the world, the more we are sinners. The more we shut ourselves off from the world, say these religions, the more holy we are.

Examples of this can be found in the largest branch of Christianity, the Roman Catholic Church. Its religious leaders—priests, monks, and nuns—are not permitted to marry. If they wish their lives to be truly holy, they may live in special buildings with little contact with the outside world, following extremely strict rules. Some Catholic monks are not permitted to speak. Throughout history, some extremely pious Christians have chosen to become hermits—living totally alone, perhaps in caves, avoiding all contact with a world they think is sinful.

There are many other examples. The holy men of Hinduism try to free themselves of all desire for the world. The Buddhist monk must give up family and property. Some Muslim groups have a holiday each year when they cut themselves with knives and pull out their hair.

All this is totally foreign to Judaism.

Many religions teach the joys of giving up the world. (Left) A young Roman Catholic nun, who has taken a vow never to marry or to own property, sits in solitary prayer. (Right) A Buddhist monk who has turned his back on worldly matters meditates on eternity.

Enjoyment—with Responsibility

Judaism has, however, avoided the other extreme: wild, riotous, or harmful activities that might for a moment seem "fun." We are to enjoy the world—but responsibly.

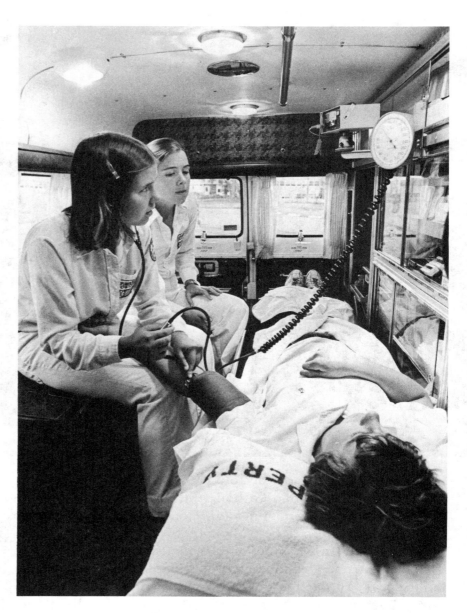

Drug abuse, which may result in overdose and even death, shows a desperate search for enjoyment with no sense of responsibility. This is not a Jewish approach to the wonders of God's world.

We are to enjoy food. Many of our happiest holidays have special, delicious recipes to help us celebrate! But we must not eat so much that we make ourselves sick, or endanger our health.

We may enjoy wine. We are frequently commanded to praise God, "who creates the fruit of the vine." But we are not to become alcoholics. Nor are we allowed to become dependent on dangerous drugs, which may destroy our brains and our bodies. Such extremes are totally forbidden.

Belief in God's Plan

Each Jew, then, is asked to view the world in an optimistic way. Each is asked to find a reasonable and responsible way to enjoy God's world.

Yet how can we feel so good about the world when there are so many things wrong with it? There is sickness and ugliness, poverty and hunger, war and pollution.

Judaism does not ask us to blind ourselves to these problems. Quite the contrary—the optimism of Judaism tells us that we can do something about them. While some faiths view the world as hopeless, Judaism says that it can be improved— and that we as individuals *can* make a difference in bringing about that improvement. Our religion tells us we should perform the deeds of righteousness that will help create a day of peace and justice for all:

> Learn to do good.
> Devote yourself to justice;
> Aid the wronged.
> Uphold the rights of the orphan;
> Defend the cause of the widow.
> [*Isaiah 1:17*]

Optimism—a Motor Idea

Jewish optimism has proved to be a very powerful motor idea. Because Jews believe that life is a gift from God, they have worked to preserve life. Throughout the centuries, Jews in exceptional numbers have been leading physicians. The men who found the cures for the diseases of polio and tuberculosis were both Jews.

Because Jews believe that humanity was created in God's image, they believe that all men and women have the right to freedom. Jews were early supporters of the American revolution, the struggle for the rights of all groups to live as equals in America, and have fought for liberty in many lands.

Because Jews believe that life is beautiful, they have worked to make it as beautiful as possible. An unusually high percentage of Jews is involved in the arts—many of the greatest artists, authors, and musicians are Jews.

Really Different?

Of course, many nations have achievements in these fields. There is talent in every land and every culture. Still, the percentage of Jews making important contributions to the welfare of the world is extraordinarily high. This has even been recognized by our enemies! Whenever there has been an enemy of freedom and decency and equality—from Haman in ancient times to Adolf Hitler in this century—he has almost always wished to destroy Jews and Judaism.

The dictators of the Soviet Union are the most recent in the line of tyrants who have felt threatened by the Jewish belief in freedom. After many years of struggle, the scientist Anatoly Shcharansky succeeded in obtaining permission to leave for Israel. He has dedicated himself to working for the thousands who still want to escape from Soviet oppression.

A Glorious World

Our people has outlived all these villains—and so it would be wrong to end this chapter on optimism with thoughts of them. Let us rather turn to a true hero, King David, who according to tradition, wrote many of the beautiful religious poems known as the Psalms. Some 3,000 years ago he sang of the wonders of creation, and the eighth poem in the Book of Psalms remains one of the most beautiful expressions of the Jewish view of the world:

> O Lord, our Lord,
> How glorious is Your name in all the earth! . . .
> When I behold your heavens, the work of Your fingers
> The moon and stars that You have set in place,
> What is man, that You are mindful of him?
> Mortal man, that You think of Him?
> Yet You have made him little lower than the angels,
> And have crowned him with glory and honor. . . .
> O Lord, our Lord,
> How glorious is Your name in all the earth!

Summary

Judaism is a religion which views things in a positive way. It is a religion of optimism. It believes that the world is good, and that God has given it to us to enjoy in a reasonable and responsible way. It is for us to improve the world, to make it possible for all people to enjoy the world's richness and beauty in freedom. This optimistic view is quite different from many religions, and has been a powerful motor idea for Judaism. A very high percentage of Jews can be found among those working to make the world a better and more beautiful place.

THE JEWISH YEAR

We live by a calendar which tells us not only what day it is, but also what moments in the year are important. A school calendar, for example, tells us how many days we are to study, how much time will be spent on exams, and how many days will be spent on vacation. The Jewish calendar reflects a specifically Jewish sense of time, combining a concern for the cycle of nature, the history of the Jewish people and the principles of Judaism. Here are some highlights of the Jewish year.

The blowing of the *shofar* (ram's horn) ushers in the Jewish new year, Rosh Hashanah. Unlike the secular new year, where tooting noise-makers is part of a night of silly celebration, the shofar calls on Jews to begin a 10-day period of serious thought on how to be better people and better Jews. The ten days conclude with a full day of fast and prayer on the holiest day of the Jewish year, Yom Kippur.

An Israeli family observes Sukkot in their *sukkah*. Sukkot—the Feast of Booths—was originally a fall harvest festival. This celebration of thanking God for good crops was the model for the American holiday of Thanksgiving. As with many Jewish holidays, celebration of the cycle of nature was combined with a specifically religious meaning.

Celebrating Simhat Torah at the Western Wall in Jerusalem. Simhat Torah—the last of the eight days of Sukkot—became the time to rejoice over the completion of the annual reading of the Torah.

Hanukkah and Purim each celebrate the victory of the Jews over a great power intent on destroying Judaism. Hanukkah marks the triumph of Judah Maccabbee over the Syrian Greeks in 165 B.C.E. Purim is the anniversary of the victory of Mordecai and Esther over the Persian villain Haman. Hanukkah is a time for lighting candles, playing games, and, of course, eating latkes (left). On Purim, everything is turned upside down. We have funny plays and we wear costumes—even in synagogue (right), when we read the Book of Esther and make loud noises to drown out Haman's evil name.

An Israeli family of Yemenite origin meets for the Passover Seder. In ancient Israel there were two spring harvests—an early harvest of barley and, seven weeks later, a harvest of wheat. The celebration of these important harvests was connected with two key events in Jewish history: the Exodus (the escape of the Jews from Egypt under the leadership of Moses) and the giving of the Torah at Mount Sinai. These are the holidays of Passover and Shavuot.

Beautiful as are the holidays which come once a year, the most remarkable Jewish holiday is the Sabbath, which comes every week. Rest became a form of religious observance. Other ancient peoples could not understand this. They thought that Jews were just lazy! Yet this idea of the Jewish calendar has transformed the calendars of the world.

6 THE JEWISH REVOLUTION

No days off!

You, and your parents, might be working seven days a week, every week of the year. If you were poor or sick or out of work, there might be no one to help you. You might be serving in an army in a society dedicated to the glories of war.

All this might have happened if you had lived before the Jewish revolution.

A Day of Rest

We think that it is normal to have time off. Every student and every worker expects weekends free of study or work.

But if you think about it, there is nothing normal about free time. A student might learn more by studying seven days a week. A company might make more profit if its workers were on the job every day.

That is the way the world was before the Jewish revolution. All but the wealthy worked practically every day of their lives. Few children had the chance to go to school. Most had to work every day beside their parents.

This was perfectly normal in those days. The Torah, however, wasn't concerned with what was *normal*—it told the world what was *right*.

Six Days You Shall Labor . . .

The Torah commands a day of rest every week. It was seen as a part of God's basic plan for the world, for

> in six days the Lord made heaven and earth, and on the seventh day He rested. [*Exodus 20:11*]

The seventh day was not just to be a day for people to relax their bodies. It was also a time to celebrate the creation, to re-

member God and His wonders. It was a time to restore tired hearts and souls, as well as tired arms and legs.

The Fourth of the Ten Commandments makes this very clear:

Six days you shall labor and do all your work, but the seventh day is the Sabbath, sacred to the Lord your God.
[*Exodus 20:9–10*]

It was normal in the early part of this century for immigrant families—children as well as parents—to slave under awful working conditions. Jews were prominent leaders in the fight for workers' rights and the creation of an extra holiday to honor laborers—Labor Day.

The Needy

Some people do not worry about vacations—they worry about being able to work. There may be no employment available, or they may be too sick to keep a job.

Often the rich and powerful have sneered at the less fortunate: "These people must be lazy. If they wanted to work, they could find work. If they took good care of themselves, they wouldn't be sick."

Part of the Jewish revolution was to say: "Many people are poor and sick and it is not their fault. They have a *right* to be helped. And it is the *duty* of everyone to help the less fortunate."

CHARITY AND TZEDAKAH: WHAT IS THE DIFFERENCE?

The English word for giving to others is *charity*, from a Latin word meaning "kindness."

The Hebrew word for giving to others is *tzedakah*.

It is the Hebrew word for "righteousness."

Is there a difference between helping someone out of *kindness* and helping someone as an act of *righteousness*?

How do you feel about a person when you are being *kind*? How do you feel about something if you do it because it is *right*?

Do you think one way is better than the other? Discuss this in class.

The Torah has many laws to protect the poor. For example, farmers may not harvest the corners of their fields. The grain from those areas is not be sold. It is to be left for the poor to gather for their own use so that they too can eat.

Note that the farmers do not give this grain to the poor as an act of kindness. Farmers must do it because the grain belongs to the poor by right. The poor should not have to ask for it. Judaism protects both the lives and the self-respect of the poor.

War

Sometimes war cannot be avoided. America needed a war to win its freedom from England, and another to end the evils of slavery.

When the United Nations voted to establish the State of Israel, the Arab countries surrounding the new Jewish nation sent in five armies to destroy it. The Israelis had no choice but to fight for their lives.

But we would rather have peace. We want a government that will try to keep us out of war.

We think of this desire for peace as normal. But it was not normal before the Jewish revolution.

Peace and War in Ancient Times

Kings were often warriors. Their greatest pride was their victories. The walls of their tombs were covered with pictures showing them in battle. Monuments were set up with inscriptions boasting of the peoples the king had conquered.

The claims made in these inscriptions were often far from true. The first reference to the people of Israel outside the Bible appears in just such an inscription, made to honor a pharaoh 3,200 years ago:

> The kings are overthrown,
> Not one holds up his head . . .
> The people of Israel is laid waste,
> It has no more children.

A statement that a pharaoh destroyed the people of Israel 32 centuries ago was certainly wishful thinking! But the point is, the pharaoh *wanted* it to be true. He wanted to be remembered as a man who could destroy other nations.

A New Vision

The Bible shows a very different view. In Judaism, a major goal is to create world peace. The prophet Isaiah does not dream of a nation with an all-powerful army. Instead, he pictures a day when armies will not be needed at all:

Ancient kings wished to be remembered as mighty warriors. In this wall painting from the Tomb of the Egyptian Pharaoh Tut-ankh-amun, troops follow their king into battle as enemy soldiers are crushed by the wheels of his chariot.

The Isaiah Wall at the United Nations complex, New York City. When the founders of the United Nations looked for a statement of their goal of world peace, they turned to the Hebrew Bible and the beautiful words of the prophet Isaiah.

Jewish history and ideals inspired the leaders of the American revolution. They chose to inscribe the liberty bell with words from our Torah: "Proclaim liberty throughout the land unto all the inhabitants thereof."

In the days to come
Many nations shall say,
"Come, let us go up to the mountain of the Lord . . .
And He will teach us His ways,
And we will walk in His paths.
For out of Zion shall go forth the Torah,
And the word of the Lord from Jerusalem. . . .
They shall beat their swords into plowshares
And their spears into pruninghooks.
Nation shall not lift up sword against nation—
They shall never again know war."

[*Isaiah 2:4*]

Where Credit is Due

We live in a land of freedom. We enjoy weekends and vacations. We see the fine work done by many charities. Our nation tries to live in peace.

We usually take all this for granted. "It's normal," we may say. If we think about it at all, we realize that people of many different religions have worked to create liberty in America, to pass laws that will protect our workers, and to promote the goal of world peace.

What we should also remember, however, is that it was Jews who brought these ideas to the world. It was the prophets and teachers of the Jewish people who taught these ideas when they were totally new and revolutionary.

Those other revolutionaries—the men who founded the

United States—*did* remember the role of the Jewish people in world history. John Adams, a leader in America's war for independence and our second president, wrote: "The Hebrews have done more to civilize men than any other nation."

A Task to Complete

Obviously our Jewish revolution is not complete. Our ideals are often unrealized, even in the United States. In some countries, they are totally ignored. There the poor are left to find their own ways to survive. They may have to spend all their time begging or sifting through garbage in the hope of finding something to eat.

Every newspaper tells us of people and nations who believe in bloodshed and violence rather than brotherhood and peace.

Still, Judaism teaches us that our hopes for the future will be realized. And each of us can play a part in making the world better. As a rabbi said nearly 2,000 years ago:

It is not your duty to complete the work, but neither are you free to give up trying. [*Pirke Avot 2:21*]

Summary

Many things that seem normal to us were once revolutionary ideas, brought to the world by the prophets and teachers of Judaism. These include the Sabbath, with a weekly time of rest; concern for the poor and helpless; and the dream of world peace. It is the duty of Jews to help make these goals realities.

It is a Jewish duty to improve the world. At the "Good Fence" along the Israel-Lebanon border, an Israeli tent clinic welcomes Lebanese families who have crossed the border seeking medical help.

7 BRANCHES

A tree must stand on firm ground and develop a solid trunk before it can put out strong branches. Judaism may be thought of in a similar way. The firm ground on which it stands is the belief in one God who has a special relationship with the Jewish people, and who has given us a homeland in Israel.

The solid trunk is formed by the teachings of Judaism: a way of life built on concern for the poor, love of peace, a sacred time for rest, the dream of building a world closer to perfection.

Now it is time to consider the different "branches" of Judaism which complete the "tree."

Jews by Country

One way that Jews branch out is by country. Jews have lived all over the world. In each land, they have developed special customs.

Trees, used in this chapter to symbolize Judaism, also play an important part in it. Each roller of a Torah scroll (seen being prepared at left in an Israeli workshop), is called an *etz chayim*—tree of life. At right, one more tree is added to the more than 135,000,000 planted to restore the ancient soil of Israel.

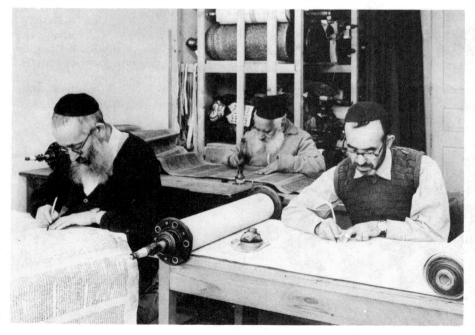

For example: in America we tend to make Ḥanukkah quite an important holiday. Some families give presents on each of the eight nights that we celebrate the victory of Judah Maccabee in the world's first war for religious freedom.

The Jews of Afghanistan think that Shavuot is one of the most important holidays, since it celebrates God's giving us the Torah. They call it the "Feast of Roses," probably because children shower the Torah with roses as the scrolls are carried in the synagogue. The Jews of Persia (now Iran) have regarded Purim as the most important holiday, since Esther, the heroine of the Purim story, was Queen of Persia. Boys run and jump through bonfires, symbolizing the escape from the fires of Haman's persecution centuries ago.

In every nation in which they lived, Jews developed their own way of eating. When Americans think of "Jewish food" they think of blintzes and herring, matzoh balls and gefilte fish—but these are really typical foods of Eastern Europe and Russia. The Jews of Italy eat spaghetti and pizza. Those in Latin America eat tacos and tortillas. Jews of Israel enjoy Middle Eastern foods like felafel and hummus.

Jews by Custom

In America, we usually speak of the three branches of Judaism: Orthodox Judaism, Conservative Judaism, and Reform Judaism. But this does not give a complete picture. Each of these three has its own special categories.

There are several forms of Orthodox Judaism. Most Orthodox Jews in this country wear modern American clothes and wear their hair in modern American styles. There are other Orthodox Jews, however, who look very different from most Americans.

Best known are the Hasidim. Their traditions were begun in Poland in the 1700's by the Baal Shem Tov, a man who believed in worshipping with dance, poetry, and a great deal of emotion. This style of worship is preserved by the Hasidim. In addition, they preserve the types of dress that were stylish two centuries ago, when Hasidism was born. These include long black coats and expensive fur hats for the Sabbath and holidays which are worn even in the heat of summer.

Conservative Judaism also has divisions. A famous Conservative rabbi had some special ideas about Judaism, and created a branch of our religion called Reconstructionism. It asks us to see Judaism as such a complete part of our lives that it led to the creation of Jewish Community Centers where even basketball and swimming could take place in a Jewish environment.

There is considerable variety in the way Jews worship, even within the same branch of Judaism. The oldest synagogue in the United States —the beautiful Touro Synagogue in Newport, Rhode Island—is built in the Spanish style with the desk for reading the Torah in the middle of the room, at a distance from the Ark.

Reform synagogues worship differently from Orthodox and Conservative Jews, but also differ widely among themselves. Some Reform congregations are traditional, while others experiment with quite untraditional ceremonies.

Surface Differences

Is it possible, then, to say what the real differences are between Orthodox, Conservative, and Reform Judaism? If you ask this question, most people will talk to you about customs. You may be told: "Orthodox and Conservative Jews wear hats when they pray. Many Reform Jews don't." Or you may hear:

The Jewish Theological Seminary in New York City, which trains Conservative rabbis, also has one of the world's greatest collections of Jewish books and manuscripts.

Mordecai Kaplan, a rabbi and professor at the Jewish Theological Seminary, founded the movement of Judaism known as Reconstructionism.

The ordination of a Reform rabbi at the Hebrew Union College in New York. Reform Judaism was the first group in modern times to permit women to serve as rabbis.

FAITH—AND BLIND FAITH

Orthodox Jews believe that the Torah is the exact word of God, but they do not believe that every statement in the Torah has only its most obvious meaning.

For example, the first chapters of the Torah tell us that the world was created in six days. "But," says the Orthodox Jew, "this does not mean six days in our sense of the word. Who knows what a day is to God? Scientists have proved that the earth developed over billions of earth years. This is no problem. It proves the obvious—that God's view of time is broader than ours."

There are people who believe that holy writings are to be taken *exactly as written*. To them, six days of creation means just that: six periods of twenty-four hours. These people are called *Fundamentalists*. There are few Jewish Fundamentalists, but there are many Christian Fundamentalists in America who wish to see the "six Days of Creation" story taught in the public schools as fact.

"Orthodox Jews won't drive a car on the Sabbath. Most Conservative and Reform Jews will."

These statements are true. But you probably realize that they do not give the complete picture. No one would bother to create a new branch of a religion just because of a hat or a car.

The Real Division

The real division among Jews has to do with the way we think about the Torah.

Orthodox Jews believe that the Torah is *the exact word of God*. The Torah we read is the very text given to Moses at Mount Sinai. The correct interpretation of the Torah was also given to Moses, and was passed on from generation to generation until it was written down in the Talmud. The Torah and the Talmud are, for the Orthodox Jew, God's complete message to humanity.

Conservative and Reform Jews believe differently. They feel that the Torah and Talmud were *inspired* by God, but were actually written by human beings over a long period of time. Because of that, they show a changing view of God, as from century to century people learned more about God's will. Some old ideas may no longer be useful in the Twentieth Century. Recent ideas may be very important. Every generation must be prepared to learn more and more about God's plan for humanity.

An Example—the Orthodox View

Because of this difference of opinion, Jews often look at new situations in opposite ways.

For example, driving a car: Should it be permitted on Shabbat, when the Torah clearly states that no work is allowed?

Orthodox Jews assume that the answer can be found in the Torah and Talmud. The Torah tells us that work is forbidden. One of the types of forbidden work is lighting a fire.

When we turn the key to start a car, we set off a spark and start a kind of fire inside the engine. This fire must continue if the car is to run. There is nothing in our sacred books to suggest that any special kind of fire should be permitted.

The Orthodox decision is to forbid starting or riding in a car on the Sabbath. Orthodox Jews walk to services.

The Same Example—Conservative and Reform Views

Conservative and Reform Jews take another approach to driving on the Sabbath.

They assume that people, not God, wrote the Torah. While God may know everything, humans do not, so the people that wrote our sacred books never imagined such a thing as an automobile. The idea of a day of rest, however, was truly inspired. It is for us to decide how to capture the *spirit* of a day of rest in light of modern conditions.

For most of us, it is far more restful to drive than to walk to a distant synagogue. So Reform Jews and most Conservative Jews approve of driving cars to services. Many Conservative Jews will not drive to other places on Shabbat, while most Reform Jews will drive freely.

Traditions—Hats or No Hats

Religion is not only laws—it is also traditions. Some traditions have become important to people, even though they are not based on the Torah and Talmud.

An example is whether or not men should wear some kind of hat when they pray. This is not stated in our sacred books. In fact, it was only a few hundred years ago (not very long in Jewish history!) that it became the custom in Europe for Jewish men to wear head coverings at all times.

About 150 years ago, the people who began Reform Judaism considered this custom from a new point of view. They realized that, in the ancient world, people *covered* their heads as a sign of respect. It made sense for these Jews to cover their heads in prayer as a sign of respect for God. But in the mod-

THE JEWS OF ETHIOPIA

Most traditional Jews believe that the Talmud is an essential guide to understanding the Torah. In Ethiopia, however, a group of black-skinned Jews became cut off from the rest of the Jewish world, and knew nothing of the Talmud. For centuries, they thought they were the only Jews left on earth! So they developed their own traditions for obeying the Torah. Here they are shown in one of their synagogues during a prayer service.

ern world, we *take* hats *off* as a sign of respect. (If a man enters a courtroom, he does not wear a hat.) So, said the Reform leaders, modern Jews should show the same respect to God, praying with heads uncovered.

Some years later, Conservative Judaism began in the United States among Jews who felt that Reform had gone too far. True, they said, there might be no logical reason to wear a hat while praying. Still, it is an honored Jewish custom—a tradition that connects us to our parents and grandparents and great-grandparents.

The leaders of a Jewish community, at right, meet a Christian king, his bishops and knights. In the Middle Ages, Jews were often forced to wear a special hat—much like what we might call a "dunce cap"— in public. In private, they might not wear a hat at all. The issue of wearing or not wearing a hat, when given the choice, is a relatively recent debate.

One of the differences between Conservative and Reform Judaism is that Conservative Jews are much more interested in "conserving" the traditions of the Jewish past.

So Conservative men do wear hats while praying. Today, many Reform Jews also wear a head covering at services to connect themselves with tradition.

Strength in Differences

Sometimes Jews get very angry when other Jews don't do things "their way." Reform Jews may think Orthodox and Conservative Jews are old-fashioned. Conservative Jews may feel that Reform and Orthodoxy each go too far. Orthodox Jews, proud in their belief that they follow God's law exactly, may sometimes feel that others are not observing an authentic Judaism.

It is too bad that Jews ever behave this way. In reality, the variety within Judaism has given it strength. Jews of different beliefs and tastes can find a branch with which they can be comfortable, and which connects them to the basic views which Jews throughout the world share.

A Tree of Life

The branches of a tree permit it to have a beautiful crown of leaves providing cooling shade to people who stand beneath it. The tree branches also give the plant the ability to bend and move in times of heavy wind and stormy weather.

The branches of the "Jewish tree" let our religion bring its benefits to a wide variety of people. They have helped Juda-

KASHRUT

Tucked away in the kitchen of a Russian Jewish family are facilities for the production of kosher wine. The dietary laws, or *kashrut*, have been an important part of Judaism since biblical times. Today Jews differ in their interpretation of *kashrut*. But all agree that Judaism, as a complete way of life, requires us to be aware of our heritage—and our obligations to God and to each other—even in every day activities such as eating and drinking. In the Soviet Union, where Jews are not permitted to practice their religion, keeping kosher becomes a heroic act of identification with Judaism and the Jewish people.

While Jews differ on various questions, they remain united on basic values, such as the safety of their fellow Jews in other countries. Here American Jews come together to protest the treatment of Jews in the Soviet Union.

ism survive under many different and sometimes difficult conditions. And they have connected Jews to the most essential part of our "tree"—the Torah. In the words of the Bible, repeated each time the Torah is read in the synagogue:

> It is a tree of life to them that hold fast to it
> And its supporters are happy.
> Its ways are ways of pleasantness
> And all its paths are peace.
>
> [*Proverbs 3:18, 17*]

Summary

Judaism can be thought of as a tree dividing into branches. These branches can be seen as expressing the many countries in which Jews have lived, or as expressing the various customs different Jews have developed. In America, we usually speak of Orthodox, Conservative, and Reform as the three branches of Judaism. These groups vary in the way they view the origin of the Torah, and in certain traditions. The variations within Judaism have strengthened our religion over the centuries.

JEWS AROUND THE WORLD

What does a Jew look like? As these pictures show, there is no "typical" Jew. Here is a gallery of Jewish faces from all around the world.

Israeli soldier

Iranian mother and child

Ethiopian immigrants in Israel

Tunisia

U.S.S.R.

Israel

PART THREE
RELIGIONS OF EAST ASIA

8 HINDUISM

At about the time of Abraham, the people of India began to develop a new religion. Today its followers number some 462,000,000—almost 1 of every 10 people in the world.

The religion is called *Hinduism*.

And it contradicts almost everything that we believe about religion and the world.

God or gods

We consider it natural to believe in one God. The Hindu heavens are said to teem with 330 million gods!

If you go to India, you will find the land covered with Hindu shrines, each containing statues of gods. Some are human in form, though they may have many arms. Some of the gods are in animal form—perhaps an elephant or a cow. Many of the shrines are very ornate, filled with colorful paintings and carvings.

Hindus bring offerings of food or flowers or money to these shrines. Often the people treat the images as if they were human. In one temple, the statue is thought to catch a cold when it is given a bath.

Many Beliefs

This does not mean that all Hindus are polytheistic. Some Hindus believe that millions of different gods truly exist, while others feel that the many gods are only images of the many aspects of one God. And some Hindus believe in no gods at all.

While we think it is natural for people of the same religion to hold many of the same beliefs, this is not the view of Hindus. Hinduism has a wide range of beliefs, dozens of branches, and hundreds of different sets of rituals. To an outside observer, Hinduism seems more like a group of religions than one single faith.

A statue of the elephant-faced Ganesha, one of the many gods of the Hindus.

The World View

Yet there is one very important belief that binds Hindus together. It is this: the world we know is not very important.

Everything in the world changes. The mountains crumble. Living things die. All we touch, all we hear, all we see, is—for the Hindu—just an illusion.

This includes our belief in ourselves. We think we know who we are, and that we are special. We look in a mirror and we see what we look like.

Yet, says the Hindu, that too is an illusion. We know that others see us very differently. To the Hindu, our notion that our own lives are somehow special is quite wrong.

The Goal of Life

The Hindu sees himself as if he were a bubble of foam on the ocean, bouncing along from wave to wave. The bubble is really useless all by itself. Bouncing along, it is blown by the wind and beaten by the rain. Only when the bubble pops and disappears, its bit of moisture blending with the ocean, does it really become part of the great water which encircles the earth.

Humans should lose their identity in just that way, says

YOGI, SWAMI, AND GURU

A Hindu holy man sits by the banks of a sacred river in a yoga position. Actually, the word *yoga* means "path" or "discipline." Hinduism teaches that there are four different paths to the goal of Nirvana: The Way of Works, The Way of Knowledge, The Way of Devotion, and The Way of Concentration. It is the last, called *Raja-yoga*, that has become well-known in the west by the shortened name of *yoga*. A *yogi*, or one who practices *yoga*, strives to control the physical body through exercises in posture, breathing, and meditation. Through these exercises the *yogi* hopes to achieve enlightenment—to lose his individual self and unite with the one great soul of the universe.

Another kind of Hindu holy man is the *swami*. Like the *yogi*, the *swami* turns his back on the normal world of business, family, and possessions. He tries to live his life as an inspiring example to other Hindus.

A *yogi* or a *swami* can also be a *guru*—another word that has become popular in the West. *Guru* is simply a title for a religious teacher.

Hinduism. The goal of our existence is to blend our souls into the great spirit of the universe. This extinction of individual life is called *Nirvana*.

This seems strange to us. We have been brought up to be concerned for everyone as an individual. We think of each person as unique and important. When our loved ones die, we mark their graves and carve their names in stone or bronze to preserve their identities.

The Hindu finds all this absurd. The Hindu wants to disappear. When he dies, he wants his body burned, and the ashes scattered in a sacred river.

Rebirth

If life is so meaningless, if only the end of life is glorious, why go on living? Why not commit suicide and end it all?

Because, according to Hinduism, death does not end it all. Our souls are reborn again and again in the bodies of other living things. This process of rebirth is called *reincarnation*.

In what kind of living thing will we reappear? That depends on how we have lived our lives. Goodness is rewarded by a higher place on the scale of living things. Evil is punished by rebirth at a lower level.

The Hindu sees each life as a bubble of foam, waiting to lose its identity in the universe.

The Hindu believes that the souls of all living beings are part of the same universal soul. Hinduism, therefore, has reverence for all forms of life. Most pious Hindus are vegetarians. Cows are viewed as so sacred that they are permitted to wander freely through the streets of most Indian cities.

The soul of a murderer might reappear in a pig or a goat. The soul of a faithful dog might be reborn in a human being. A particularly righteous soul may be reborn as a cow (a sacred animal in Hinduism).

Only the highest type of human can hope, at death, to escape from this endless cycle of rebirths and merge into the spirit of the universe.

The Caste System

We say "the highest type of human," for Hinduism sees humanity divided into several different classes. One of its key teachings is that humanity is not basically united, but divided into separate and separated levels.

Each level is called a *caste*. The highest of these is the priestly caste. Its members enjoy many privileges. Below them stand the kings and warriors. Third comes the caste of merchants and laborers.

Priests, merchants, and laborers exist in most societies, of course, but in Hinduism they are truly separated. Each caste has its own rules and its own activities. In traditional Hinduism, it is impossible to move from one caste to another.

This is especially true for the people at the very bottom level of society: the *untouchables*. According to Hindu tradition, an untouchable could not walk on the street near a member of a higher caste. An untouchable could not even permit his shadow to fall on a member of a higher caste! He could justify his existence only by doing the very dirtiest work.

Motor Ideas: Caste System

The idea of "caste" is a key motor idea of Hinduism.

It teaches that the inequalities of life are an exact reflection of what a person has earned, based on what he did in a former life. Any attempt to change things for the better is a terrible mistake.

A poor man deserves his poverty. It is wrong to try to help him, for he deserves whatever happens to him.

Our ideals of charity make little sense to the Hindus.

The Place of Women

Hindu society is traditionally male-oriented. The duty of a woman is clear: to serve her husband. If her husband died, she was never to remarry. In fact, tradition held that, when his corpse was burned, she was to throw herself on the funeral pyre and unite with him, to join him in his next reincarnation.

Gandhi

Some of these views have changed in modern times. Mohandas Gandhi, a Hindu who was educated in Britain, brought back to India the concept that humans should be treated as equals. Thanks to his work, the idea of untouchability was outlawed. Women are no longer expected to be mere servants of their husbands, or to commit suicide when their husbands die. In fact, for many years India was led by a Prime Minister who was a woman and a widow.

These changes have not come easily. There has been much resistance from traditional Hindus. Gandhi himself was murdered by a traditional Hindu who felt the changes coming to India were a betrayal of Hinduism.

Two Pure Forms

In traditional Hinduism and traditional Judaism, we see the two opposite poles of religion.

Hinduism is a religion of pessimism. It says that the world is meaningless. It insists that souls are doomed to an almost endless round of rebirths into this world of misery. And there is nothing we can or should do to improve the world. The caste into which we are born reflects the reward or punishment for our previous lives. It is our duty to accept things as they are.

Judaism is a religion of optimism. It says that the world is good, and life is good; and that since we have only one life we

Mohandas Gandhi led India to independence from Great Britain through non-violent resistance. He worked to change India, gaining rights for women and "untouchables."

The Mukteshwar Temple in northeastern India. Like the religion they represent, Hindu temples can be overwhelming in grandeur and baffling in their complexity. Each carving has its own meaning, so that the temple becomes a symbol in stone of the entire universe.

JUDAISM AND HINDUISM

A comparison of Judaism and Hinduism shows that they represent the opposite poles of religion.

	JUDAISM	HINDUISM
General mood	Optimistic	Pessimistic
God	One	Millions
The world is	Good	Bad
Humans are	Equal	Divided into castes
Each lifetime is	Unique	One of a round of rebirths
Goal	To improve the world	To escape the world

should make the most of it. All humans are equal in the sight of God, and it is our duty to make life better for everyone. It is our task to help perfect the world.

Summary

While Hindusim began in India about the same time that Judaism began with Abraham in the Middle East, the two developed in totally different ways. Hinduism has many forms of belief, and millions of gods. Its unifying idea, however, is that the world as we know it is meaningless, and that we are caught in an endless cycle of rebirths into it. Our goal is to earn higher and higher levels in each rebirth, working our way through the caste system into which humanity is rigidly divided, until we can at last disappear, blending into the spirit of the universe—the state of *Nirvana*.

9 BUDDHISM

A wealthy Indian prince named Gautama became dissatisfied. He lived in luxury, and was happy with his family. Still, he realized that most people were not so fortunate. Outside his palace there were pain and suffering. He felt certain that he had to face those realities to discover truths that were hidden from him by his gold and jewels.

At the age of 29—about the year 530 B.C.E.—he left his home, his riches, his wife, and his child. He shaved his head and, dressed only in the yellow robe of a monk, set out to find the meaning of life.

Failure and Success

He was a Hindu, and so he tried Hindu ways of searching for knowledge. Hinduism taught that suffering could lead to wisdom. Gautama gave up food, almost starving himself to death. But he felt he had learned nothing.

Finally he sat under a sacred tree and vowed to sit there, thinking, until he discovered the secrets of life.

Buddhist tradition states that he remained under that tree for forty-nine days of meditation. Then, at last, he found the answers he was seeking. He found what Buddhism has called *Enlightenment*.

After that he was known as the *Buddha*—"the Enlightened One."

For the remaining forty-five years of his life, he traveled throughout northern India, gaining converts to his new religion.

Desires Lead to Unhappiness

What did the Buddha learn under the tree?

He had come to the conclusion that desires lead to unhappiness. We want good food—but then we eat too much, and

Guatama reached enlightenment after 49 days of meditation. This image of the Buddha is at the Sokkuram Grotto Shrine in South Korea.

worry about getting sick or gaining weight. We love our parents—but we know that one day they will die. We hope to live in a nice house—but then we have to pay for it, and find ways to keep out thieves.

The Buddha's solution was simple: give up the desire for anything that could make us unhappy.

This means giving up almost everything. The only desire that can bring us joy is the desire to erase all other desires.

"The Middle Way"
According to the Buddha, then, we should give up most of the things that people find most important. Food (beyond the

minimum needed to survive), money, position, family—all can be ignored.

On the other hand, we should not be like the Hindu wise men who had taught Gautama to search for truth with self-torture. He had tried finding wisdom through starvation. His attempt to learn this way had also led to unhappiness.

So, he said, one should avoid extremes. Live without seeking either great joy or great pain. Seek *The Middle Way.*

The Life of a Buddhist Monk

The Buddhist Middle Way seems anything but moderate to us. By our standards, it is extremely severe. The Buddhist monk must follow three strict rules.

Concern for Life: he is to love all humans without exception. He must not harm any living thing. One of his few pos-

A young child begins the training which will make him a Buddhist monk.

sessions is a strainer to remove bugs from his drinking water so that he will not accidentally hurt an insect.

Freedom from Attachments: he has no wife or family. He is not to look at dancing, or at dramatic performances, since these might remind him of women and family life.

Poverty: other than his strainer, he owns only his robe, a needle, a string of beads to use in meditations, a razor to shave his head, and a bowl with which to beg food. He eats only the food he is given while begging, and eats only before noon.

Nirvana

There is a great reward for the true Buddhist.

The Hindu believes that he must constantly be reborn. He must pass through hundreds, perhaps thousands, of reincarnations. He must endure countless lifetimes before he can hope to disappear into the universe and reach Nirvana.

The Buddha, on the other hand, taught that his followers could escape immediately from that cycle. By following Buddhism, they could be assured that death would be a final release. They would reach a Nirvana which he described as a perfect state of happiness and peace, free from all pain.

In many lands, Buddhism changed from a religion of the Buddha's teachings to a religion about the Buddha himself. This statue of Buddha preaching a sermon is an object of worship in Japan. It is 53 feet tall and weighs 452 tons, the largest bronze statue in the world.

A Non-Religion

To help others reach Nirvana, to free them from existence—this was the Buddha's only thought. As you can see, he did not mean to create a religion. he was not concerned with a God or gods. He was not concerned with worship or prayer. He was not interested in improving the world, or in Heaven or Hell.

His teachings were meant to help others escape from existence.

To follow his teachings was demanding and difficult—and the Buddha realized this. He hoped to reach only that small group of people willing to devote their lives to the search for self-knowledge.

The Great Change

But the masses were concerned more with the teacher than the teaching. They became fascinated with the Buddha himself. They honored the saintly prince who gave up wealth and riches to seek quiet peace, and then gave up his own peace to teach his truth to others.

Everything about the Buddha became sacred. A tooth or hair from his body would be preserved in a shrine called a *stupa* or

(Right) A Buddhist temple in northern India. Although the Buddha lived and died in India, his teachings never gained a large following there. They did, however, become extremely popular throughout the rest of eastern Asia, including Korea, where the ancient wooden temple of Popchu-sa can be found, alongside a 50-foot statue of the Buddha (left).

As Buddhism spread throughout Asia it gave birth to different sects, some of which incorporated other gods and religious ideas into their version of Buddhism. In 1266, the Tendai sect of Japan built the world's longest wooden structure to honor a goddess of mercy. It contains over one thousand images of the goddess.

pagoda. Such relics were obviously in limited supply, and so other shrines were built around pictures of the Buddha, or books of his teachings.

Statues of him were created—some tiny, some as large as a five-story house. The man who refused to own anything when he was alive is portrayed in gold and precious jewels.

The teacher who had not been interested in worship became the object of worship. The Buddha had helped people when he was alive. Surely he would still help those who prayed to him!

There are many sects of Buddhism, but in the largest, Gautama Buddha is worshipped as a god, a divine being who came to earth just to help humanity escape from its suffering.

In short, the teachings *of* the Buddha were transformed into a religion *about* the Buddha.

The Spread of Buddhism

Gautama would surely be shocked to see what had become of his teachings; but, perhaps even more, he would be amazed at how many people still listen to them. For Buddhism spread throughout Asia, and from there around the globe.

Surprisingly, Buddhism has faded away in most of India, the land where Gautama Buddha lived his entire life. In the rest of Asia, however, it is by far the most prominent religion. In its many forms, Buddhism has some 250,000,000 followers.

ZEN BUDDHISM

How would you answer these questions:

What is the sound of one hand clapping? Where there is nothing, what do we find?

Don't worry if you find these questions difficult. They're not really questions, at least not what we usually understand questions to be. They are examples of *koan*—a problem posed by Buddhist teachers to help students move beyond their normal patterns of thought. The *koan* is an essential practice of a type of Buddhism known as Zen.

Legend has it that a disciple came to the Buddha with a gift of a golden flower and asked him to explain the secret of his teaching. The Buddha took the flower and studied it without saying a single word.

The Buddha, say Zen teachers, wanted to show his disciple that some things cannot be explained in words, but can be learned only through direct personal experience. You can tell a person all about fire, but will that person really understand what fire is without seeing it, smelling it, feeling its heat?

For Zen Buddhists, enlightenment cannot be achieved through words. Words, logical descriptions of things, have nothing to do with the true nature of the universe. So a follower of Zen will try to get around logic by meditating on problems that don't seem to make much sense, such as the *koans* quoted above. They hope that through such meditation they will gain *satori*—flashes of insight that lead to enlightenment.

Most of the world's Zen Buddhists live in Japan. A few live in secluded *monasteries* (upper right), where they follow a strict schedule of work and meditation. Another form of Zen meditation is the practice of elaborate rituals with precise rhythms and very few words. One such ritual is the Tea Ceremony (lower right). Can you explain how a tea ceremony can help people achieve the goals of Zen Buddhism?

Summary

Gautama Buddha was an Indian prince who abandoned his riches and family to search for truth. After much searching, he concluded that by abandoning all desires one could free oneself from the endless cycle of rebirths (taught by Hinduism) and reach total peace, Nirvana. The masses were less concerned with his teaching than with the personality of the Buddha. Buddhism became a religion *about* the Buddha—and in this form grew to be the most widespread religion of Asia.

10 ASIAN THOUGHT

The last two chapters have given only the briefest of introductions to the major religions of East Asia. Whole books, even whole libraries, can be devoted to the ideas, the history, and the customs of Hinduism and Buddhism. We have been able to offer only the most basic facts.

Yet, in a sense, facts don't matter—at least in the sense we usually think of them. And this is very important to understand. It is not just a few ideas or customs or historical events that separate East and West. It is a whole way of looking at the world.

A World of Illusion

Remember that for the Hindu and the Buddhist this world is unimportant. It is a place of rebirth from which we must try to escape.

More than that—the world is not even real. It is what they call *Maya*—"Illusion."

You may look at a tree. You are convinced that it is there, and that you are seeing it directly. You can feel it, touch it, measure it, destroy it.

The religions of East Asia look at things quite differently. They teach a completely different attitude.

Their view suggests you can never look at a tree directly. It is as if you can only see it reflected in a pond. Everything you see is then only a *reflection of reality*. You can try to touch it, but when you do you merely stir up the water and see less than when you were doing nothing!

The whole world, they say, is something like this. We can never know true reality. What we think we see is Maya—illusion.

Ways to Deal with Maya

How, then, are we to deal with a world of illusion?

Let us go back to the image of looking at the tree in a pond. One possible reaction is to curse the pond. "It's all the pond's fault. If it weren't there, I could see the tree itself." But this proves to be silly. The pond dries up—and you see no tree at all.

Another choice is to treat the tree's reflection as if it were the real thing. But this doesn't work either. We try to measure the reflection, but the sun sets and the length of the reflection changes. We try to determine its color, and the sky turns gray, changing the color of the water.

We can give up on the whole thing. This is often the Hindu choice. "It's only illusion. Forget about it."

The pious Asian thinks of the world as an illusion, at best a reflection of a reality that cannot be seen directly.

The Asian learns to know the pond—and the world—through the practice of meditation.

Meditation

Then there is perhaps the best choice: let's look at the pond, and think about it.

Looking at the undisturbed reflection, keeping still while the water is keeping still, you can get a pretty good idea of what the tree is like. You can get some sense of what it really is, even though you cannot see it directly.

What you do see is a different kind of beauty. The changes of color as the sun rises and sets make it all but impossible to tell the true color of the tree, but are quite beautiful in themselves.

In this way, quiet thought—meditation—became an important part of Asian religion. In a world thought of as illusion, it provided a way to think about other, sometimes more beautiful realities.

Different kinds of Truths

Meditation is seen as leading to a sort of truth. This may not, however, be truth as Westerners think of it.

To Christians, for example, Jesus is the central figure of history. It is a high goal to know as many facts about him as possible. Many books have been written trying to determine the true facts of his life.

East Asians think this is a great deal of fuss about nothing. They don't see what difference it makes. If a person believes in the words Jesus is supposed to have said, what difference does it make whether or not he said them, or whether or not he ever lived?

Mixing Religions

Westerners tend to think of religions as being exclusive. Either you are a Jew or you are a Christian or you are a Muslim. You cannot be any of these and worship idols. But Easterners don't think in the same way.

As we have seen, Hindus feel they can all be part of the same

This is a garden in a Buddhist Temple in Japan. Yet it is not exactly a garden—it is a rock garden. And the small rocks have been carefully arranged to suggest water. Are we to think of it as a pond? Or is this a sea with islands in it? Are the islands Japan? Or do they represent individuals, alone in the universe? What is real, what is illusion?

religion even though some Hindus worship many gods and some worship no gods. While some worship many idols, some worship no idols.

Buddhism seems even more open-minded. In countries like Japan and China, it grew among people who already practiced their own national religions. No choice was required. A person could follow any number of religions.

This ancient Shinto shrine, located on a tiny island off the coast of Japan, is dedicated to the goddess who protects sailors. The sea washes over it at high tide, creating the unusual floating effect seen here.

Japan and China

In Japan, for example, there is an ancient religion called *Shinto*. It involves reverence for the many sacred places in Japan, for Japanese ancestors, and for the Emperor who, until the end of the Second World War, was worshipped as a descendant of the sun god.

But one does not have to follow Shinto exclusively. It is perfectly natural for a Japanese home to have a Shinto shrine in one room and a Buddhist shrine in another.

In China, there are two ancient religions. One is *Taoism* (pronounced DOW-izm), which teaches passive and quiet acceptance of the ways of the universe. The other is *Confucianism*, based on the practical teachings through which the sage Confucius set out his view of correct behavior.

Buddhism, which came to China some 600 years after these other religions developed, mixed happily with them. It was possible for a court official to be buried holding in his hands sacred writings of *all three* religions. Some said that this devotion to Buddhism, Taoism, and Confucianism made this man "a typical Chinese."

The Appeal of Asian Thought

There is much that is appealing about all this. When we rush about from school to homework to synagogue to movies to dates to television to music lessons to sports to whatever else occupies our time, almost anything that makes us stop and think for a moment has got to be helpful! And religions that say, "Don't bother to make choices, take all of us" seem to make life a lot easier than ones which say, "Choose only one. Choose me!"

It is not surprising, then, that from time to time Western countries have seen waves of interest in Eastern religions. This is probably a very good thing. It is certainly good for us to learn about religions that bring meaning to the lives of hundreds of millions of people. It is good for us too, to learn about techniques for understanding and appreciating the world—such as Hindu and Buddhist concepts of meditation. The very fact that East Asian thought is so very different from our own challenges us to re-examine our own ideas.

One must not become too romantic about Asian thought. While much of it is appealing, there are also many aspects we cannot approve of. The Hindu caste system, for example, iso-

---

BEWARE OF IMITATIONS!

Some men have taken attractive bits of Eastern religion, wrapped them in packages which pretend to offer easy solutions to world problems, and lured students into their groups.

Unlike true religious leaders, these people deceive their followers, destroy their minds, and steal their money.

These groups are known as *cults*. You will find more information about the evils of these organizations in Chapter 16.

lates people from one another; it does not at all coincide with our understanding of equality and fairness. And Asians are just as likely to ignore the teachings of their religions as are people in the West. Buddhists of China and Buddhists of Japan fought each other in wars every bit as fierce as those fought between Christians of France and Christians of Germany.

Still, there is a great fascination in learning about East Asian religions. We may believe strongly that the world exists, that we can learn to understand it, that we know who we are. But it is intriguing to think about problems such as the one which worried an ancient Chinese philosopher:

Last night I dreamed that I was a butterfly. How do I know that today I am not a butterfly dreaming that I am a man?

Summary

East Asian thought tends to be very different from that of the West. It develops from religions that say the world we see is only *Maya*—illusion. Because we see only a reflection of reality, meditation becomes a tool to search for truth. Asians combine Buddhism or Hinduism with various national religions. Few Westerners can truly accept the basic principles of Hinduism or Buddhism, but learning about these faiths can be fascinating.

CELEBRATING IN A WORLD OF ILLUSION

Although Asian religion teaches that the world we know is a world of illusion, it is still the world in which people must live. Despite the fact that much of the religious thought is pessimistic, many of the celebrations are happy and colorful.

A family celebrates *Divali*, the Hindu Festival of Light, which comes in the fall at the end of the rainy season in India. The holiday celebrates the homecoming of the god Rama after his defeat of a demon king. Lights are kindled to guide the goddess of wealth and prosperity to each home. Children put on their best clothes for the holiday, when they see fireworks and are given special treats to eat.

In Hinduism, the banks of rivers are places where heaven and earth meet. Of the rivers, the holiest is the Ganges. Hindus come by the millions to bathe in the river; they feel that they are purified by its waters.

A Shinto wedding ceremony. Before their immediate families, a bride and groom make pledges of marriage and prepare to share a ceremonial drink of sake from tiny ceramic cups. In much of Japan, Buddhism and Shinto exist side by side. It is quite common for a Japanese family to follow Shinto customs for celebrating births and marriages, and Buddhist customs for burying and remembering the dead! This mixing of religions, while strange to us, is not at all unusual in Asia.

The Buddhist ceremony of floating lanterns takes place on the night when the spirits of the ancestors are believed to rejoin the world of the living. To welcome the ancestors, small lanterns are lit by the banks of a river and floated downstream.

Shinto customs also live on in colorful public festivals such as these, where people put on traditional costumes and participate in ancient ceremonies honoring their ancestors and gods. The Shinto festival of Yayoi (right), takes place every April in the city of Nikko. (Above) The Gion festival in Kyoto. The large floats contain life-size figures of famous people from Japanese history and legend.

PART FOUR
CRESCENT AND CROSS

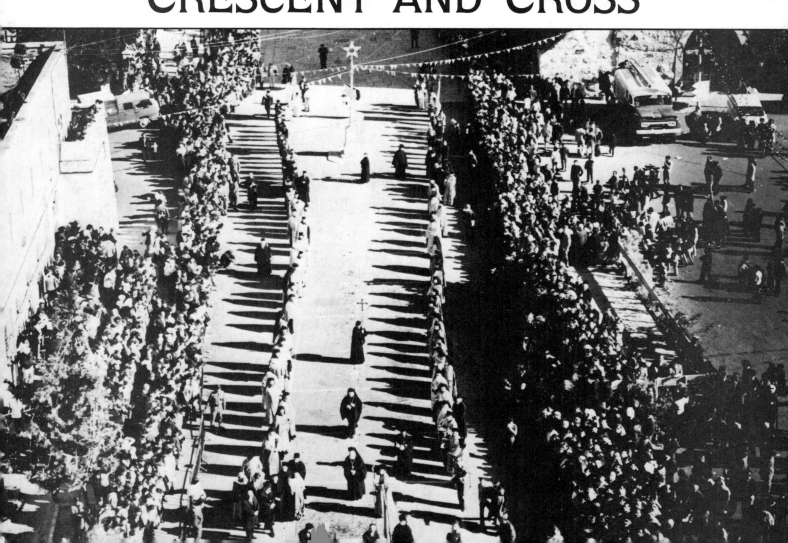

11 ISLAM

Two world religions drew their inspiration from Judaism: Christianity and Islam.

We live in a country which is predominantly Christian. We are accustomed to dealing with Christians and often enjoy items of Christian culture.

Islam is centered in faraway lands of Asia and Africa. It is the principal religion of the Arab countries which have sworn to destroy Israel, the Jewish state.

Because of all this, we often think of Judaism and Christianity as close to each other, with Islam being foreign and distant.

But in terms of belief and history, Judaism and Islam are in many ways the closest of the world's great religions.

Holy sites of Judaism and Islam are found within a few feet of each other in Jerusalem. The Western Wall is precious to Jews as the last remnant of the ancient Temple. Behind it is the Dome of the Rock, built around the stone from which, Muslims believe, their prophet Muhammad rose to heaven.

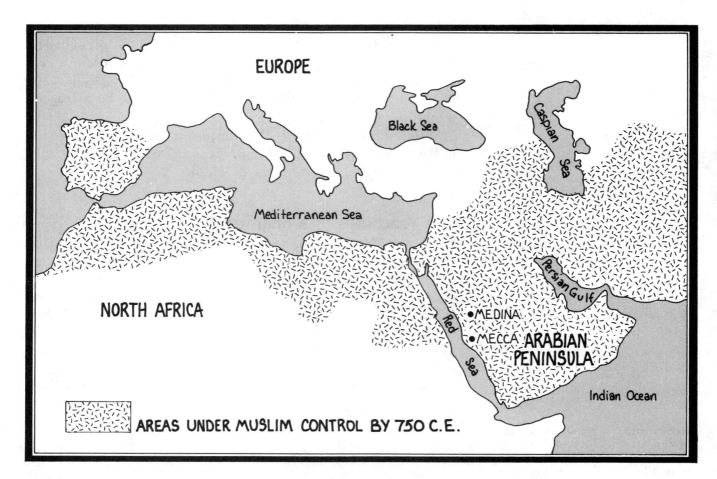

AREAS UNDER MUSLIM CONTROL BY 750 C.E.

Muhammad

This is no accident, for the great prophet of Islam—Muhammad—was deeply influenced by Judaism.

Muhammad was born about the year 570 C.E. in Arabia. In those days, the Arabs—the people of Arabia—worshipped idols, and believed in many gods and goddesses.

Since Arabia was the center of trade routes which crossed the Middle East, Jews and Christians frequently came to the desert kingdom. Many Jews made homes there. In addition, Muhammad traveled in caravans which visited the land of Israel.

With each contact, he became more impressed with Judaism and Christianity, the religions which taught of one God.

The Birth of Islam

When Muhammad was about forty, he began to have visions of an angel speaking to him. Gradually, Muhammad became convinced that he was receiving messages from the one God. This was the same God worshipped by Jews and Christians. Muhammad called this God "Allah" (a name related to a Hebrew word for God, *Elohim*.)

Muhammad's childhood trips to Palestine helped convince him of the truth of monotheism. As an adult he preached these ideas in his native city of Mecca, narrowly escaping a murder plot against him by fleeing to Medina. Muslims call this event the *hegira* ("escape"), and they begin their calendar from 622 C.E., the year it occurred. By the year 750 C.E., just over a century later, Muslim armies had conquered all of western Asia, North Africa, and most of Spain.

Inspired by the visions, Muhammad began to preach. His first sermons were given in his native city, Mecca. Many people ridiculed him. Others plotted to murder him. He fled 200 miles north, to the town of Medina, and there he attracted many followers.

Muhammad's escape to Medina in 622 C.E. is known by the Arabic word for "flight"—*hegira*. It is the event which marks the beginning of the calendar of Islam.

The Teachings of Muhammad

What were Muhammad's ideas? What did he teach that made people want to kill him?

Nothing that seems very unusual to us. He taught that there is one God. He taught that God cares whether humans are good or bad. He taught that good people would be rewarded after death with new life in paradise, while the evil would be punished for their sins. He taught that rich and poor were equal in the sight of God.

These ideas were new—revolutionary—to the idol worship-

Muhammad's visions were recorded in the sacred book of Islam—the *Koran*. It is read and studied by Muslims everywhere.

pers of Arabia. That is why Muhammad created many enemies. But the ideas weren't really new—and Muhammad didn't claim they were. He saw himself as the last and greatest of the prophets, among whom he included Adam, Noah, Abraham, Moses, and Jesus.

Christians feel that their religion brought the ideas of Judaism to completion. In the same way, Muhammad claimed that his new religion completed both Judaism and Christianity. He felt that he had brought to perfection the half-truths of the two religions that had preceded him.

The Five Pillars

One of the attractions of his teaching was that its principles were simple and clear. They are summed up in the requirements known as the *Five Pillars of Islam*. These pillars are: *Belief, Prayer, Charity, the Fast of Ramadan,* and *Pilgrimage to Mecca*.

Pillar One: Belief

"There is no God but Allah, and Muhammad is the prophet of Allah."

This is Islam's most basic teaching. It is an expression of faith which all Muslims accept, and repeat daily when they worship.

Allah is believed to have a plan for the world, and true believers must submit to it. In fact, the word *Islam* means "submission." A believer in Islam is a *Muslim*—which means "one who submits."

Muhammad is seen as a prophet, not a son of Allah or a God to be worshipped. (For this reason, Muslims are justly annoyed when others refer to their religion as "Muhammadanism.") In this respect, Islam is closer to Judaism than to Christianity, which worships Jesus as the Son of God.

Pillar Two: Prayer

A devout Muslim reserves five times a day for prayers—prayers which praise God and affirm submission to God's will.

On Fridays, public prayer is held in a building called a *mosque*. Services usually include a sermon on some aspect of Muslim law.

Muslim worship does not *look* much like Jewish worship as we know it. Muslims kneel on prayer mats or rugs, and show their submission to Allah by bowing forward, touching their foreheads to the ground. But, in fact this is how Jews bowed before the Lord in the ancient Temple, before it fell to the Romans in 70 C.E.

In what is said and done, Islam is again more like Judaism than Christianity. Judaism and Islam emphasize prayer and study. As we will see, traditional Christian worship centers on rites designed to free the worshippers from sin.

Pillar Three: Charity

Every Muslim is expected to give to other Muslims. The money is used for support of the poor, and to maintain mosques so that all may worship. Judaism also emphasizes charity—

A *mosque*, or Muslim house of worship, in Turkey. Many mosques are quite beautiful, with inlaid tiles, decorated archways, and colorful woven rugs. At the front of the mosque, on the wall closest to Mecca, is a stand reserved for the *Imam*, who leads prayers and sometimes gives a sermon.

though here the difference is significant. Judaism, but not Islam, demands care for the poor of other religions, "the stranger in your gates."

Pillar Four: The Fast of Ramadan

Muhammad had his first visions in the Arabic month of Ramadan. His visions became the basis of Islam, and the record of his visions is the holy book of Islam, the *Koran*.

For these reasons, the month of Ramadan is sacred to Muslims. It is honored by a month of fasting during daylight hours. "Eat and drink," says the Koran, "until so much of the dawn appears that a white thread may be distinguished from a black thread. Then keep the fast completely until night."

This fast includes a prohibition on drinking any sort of liquid. This can be very difficult when Ramadan falls in the dreadful heat of an Arabian summer.

(Left) Muslims prepare to enter a mosque by removing their shoes and washing their feet. This prevents the mosque from being soiled by the dirt of the outside world, and recalls God's command to Moses at the burning bush: "Remove your shoes, for the place on which you stand is holy ground."

(Right) A Muslim will pray facing the direction of Islam's most holy city, Mecca, kneeling and bowing to the ground to show submission to the will of God.

It is the duty of every Muslim to make the pilgrimage to Mecca, and to walk seven times around this shrine, the holiest of Islam. It is called the *Kabba*. It contains a rock where, according to tradition, the angel Gabriel rested his head.

Pillar Five: Pilgrimage to Mecca

Mecca had been the sacred city of Arabs since the most ancient times, centuries before Muhammad was born there. After his success in Medina, he returned to Mecca and dedicated its shrines to the worship of Allah. It has been the spiritual center of Islam ever since—the city to which each Muslim directs his prayers.

At least once in a lifetime, every Muslim—man or woman—is expected to make a pilgrimage to Mecca. Every pilgrim wears the same plain white garment, so that no one can tell who is rich or poor, powerful or peasant, as they join in celebration.

Other Teachings

Naturally, many other laws and customs have developed in Islam. Two, in particular, emphasize the closeness between

DIVISIONS

Muhammad died suddenly, without naming an heir. There was immediate disagreement over how his successor should be named, and that disagreement still divides the Muslim world.

Some 90% of all Muslims are *Sunnis*, who believe that the leaders of Islam should be nominated by representatives of the community and then confirmed by a general oath of allegiance.

Most of the remaining 10% are *Shi'ites*, who believe that authority is hereditary, passed on through Muhammad's cousin. In the absence of an heir, certain religious leaders have the power to rule.

Although they are a tiny minority of Islam, the Shi'ites are frequently in the news. They are violently opposed to the Sunnis, and to many developments of the modern world. A group of extremist Shi'ites overthrew the government of Iran and took dictatorial control. Others are believed to be responsible for much world-wide terrorism.

Judaism and Islam. Like traditional Jews, Muslims do not eat pork, and they strictly forbid graven images—representations of the human form in art. Unlike traditional Christian churches, which have paintings and sculptures of Jesus and of saints, mosques are decorated only with abstract designs, and with quotations from the Koran written in beautiful Arabic lettering.

Jihad

One of Muhammad's ideas was unique. This was the concept of the *jihad*—the "holy war." Muhammad taught that it was a sacred duty to fight for Islam. Anyone who died fighting for the faith would go directly to a heaven filled with unending delights.

The Arabs responded with an energy and enthusiasm that swept away every enemy they met. Within a century of Muhammad's death, the Arabs had conquered the land of Israel, all of North Africa, Spain, and Asia as far as India.

Jews and Muslims

Jews in most of these countries had been living under the rule of evil tyrants. Our ancestors were delighted to be freed from suffering, and welcomed the Muslims as liberators.

You might think that, with so many similarities between Judaism and Islam, Jews and Muslims would have lived to-

MAIMONIDES AND THE "GOLDEN AGE"

During the "Golden Age," Jews and Muslims worked together to create a magnificent culture. At a time when even the kings in Christian Europe could hardly write their names, Muslim society boasted brilliant scholars and excellent libraries. In this world, Jews often rose to high positions. Of these, the most brilliant was Moses Maimonides (honored by this statue in Cordova, the Spanish city where he was born). He was such a great physician that he was appointed to serve in the Sultan's court. At the same time, he led the Jewish community in Egypt and wrote Jewish books of such value that they are still studied today.

gether fairly peacefully. For many centuries, they did. Judaism has always looked back to the period from about 800 to 1200 C.E. as a time when Jews under Muslim rule enjoyed a "Golden Age."

That Golden Age is the one truly bright spot in Jewish history following the destruction of the Second Temple. Until modern times it was the period when Jews were most free, most prosperous, most productive, and made the greatest contribution to the society in which they lived. At one time, a Jew was even the top-ranking general of a kingdom in Muslim Spain!

Today, many Muslims live in the State of Israel. They enjoy complete freedom of religion. They are citizens of the state, vote in its elections, and have chosen their own representatives to sit in the Israeli parliament.

Unfortunately, there is also the dark side of the picture. Over the centuries, many Muslim rulers treated their Jewish subjects with great cruelty. When the State of Israel was created, Arab armies immediately invaded it. Today, all Arab countries except Egypt remain committed to destroying the Jewish State. Most other Muslim countries usually support this position.

Islam Today

Islam is truly a world religion. Most Arabs—people whose ancestors came from Arabia—follow the religion created by the Arab Muhammad. His followers were so successful at spreading his faith, however, that today Arabs are only one part of the Muslim world. Turkey, Malaysia, Iran, Pakistan, and Bangla-

desh are some of the non-Arabic Muslim countries. Russia has a Muslim population of 50 million. The largest Muslim state is Indonesia, with more than 100 million non-Arab Muslim citizens.

Yet, wherever they live, whatever their background, Muslims pray in Arabic and study the Koran in Arabic. Arabic is to the Muslim what Hebrew is to the Jew.

The Islamic world has major divisions. It has a number of sects, some violently opposed to each other.

Nevertheless, the words of Muhammad continue to inspire nearly one-seventh of the total population of the earth. Each

The "Golden Age" of relations between Muslims and Jews is long gone. This new arch frames the ruins of the Hurvan Synagogue, one of many Jewish sites destroyed by the Muslims of Jordan when they controlled the Old City of Jerusalem (1948–1967).

THE BAHA'I FAITH

In the 1800's, a new religion split off from Islam. Called *Baha'i*, it emphasizes the unity of all religions, world peace, and equality of men and women. Faced with violent oppression in Iran, the country where Baha'i was founded, it has established its world headquarters in Haifa, Israel, where it maintains this beautiful temple and garden.

The El Aksa Mosque in Jerusalem, close by the Dome of the Rock. Note the slim domed tower, called a *minaret*. A typical mosque has one or more of them. Five times a day an offical of the mosque—called a *muezzin*—climbs to the top of the *minaret* to call to faithful Muslims and remind them of the hour of prayer. In some places today, mechanization has changed this system. Instead of the *muezzin* a tape recorder, linked to a time-clock and a loudspeaker, punctually summons the faithful to worship.

day, half a billion people turn toward Mecca to proclaim:

"There is no God but Allah, and Muhammad is the prophet of Allah."

Summary

Muhammad created the religion of Islam. Although raised in Arab polytheism, he believed that his visions made him the last and greatest of the Jewish prophets. Many of his teachings were similar or identical to Judaism: belief in one God, prayer, charity, the prohibition of pork, opposition to all forms of idolatry. Some ideas were quite different, such as the required pilgrimage to Mecca and the Fast of Ramadan. Particularly significant was his concept of *jihad*—a holy war to spread the faith. Muhammad's followers conquered much of the known world. About one-seventh of the world's population is now Muslim. At certain periods, Muslims have lived peacefully and productively with Jews—a situation which, unfortunately, does not exist today.

12 THE BIRTH OF CHRISTIANITY

Jews have known many triumphs during the 4,000 years of our history.

We have also known many tragedies.

One of these tragedies was the conquest of Eretz Yisrael by the armies of Rome in 63 B.C.E. Roman governors were placed in control of the country, and many of them were horribly cruel. They murdered innocent men, women, and children. They stole golden treasures from the Temple in Jerusalem. They tried to prevent Jews from worshipping God.

The Jews prayed for someone who would save them from the power of Rome.

What Kind of Savior?

Save them from Rome? Rome was the center of an empire that was the most powerful on earth! What kind of a savior could gain freedom for the tiny land of Israel?

He would be an extraordinary soldier. In fact, to be such an extraordinary soldier he would have had to be sent by God for the purpose of liberating the Jewish people. But this man would be human—not a god or the child of a god.

Having freed the country, he would rebuild it. He would reestablish the kingdom of Israel and rule as king. This meant he would be a member of the Jewish royal house—a descendant of King David.

The ceremony of creating a Jewish king involved "anointing"—placing holy oil on his head. Therefore the new king would be "the anointed one." In Hebrew, the word for "anointed one" is *mashiach*. In English, this became *Messiah*.

The Messiah would be no ordinary ruler. He would bring the country, and perhaps the world, the era of peace and justice of which the Biblical prophets had spoken.

A soldier thought by many Jews to be the Messiah was Simon Bar Kochba, who led a revolt against Rome in 132 C.E. He held off the Roman armies for three years—during which he wrote letters such as this one, preserved in the dry climate of Israel for nearly 2,000 years. But his rebellion was crushed.

Crucifixion (death on a cross) was the normal Roman method of executing rebels. Others were executed in this way along with Jesus, as is shown in this fifteenth-century painting by Jan van Eyck. But the crucifixion of Jesus was to change the history of the world.

Expecting the Last Judgment

In many centuries and in many lands, oppressed Jews have identified someone as the Messiah, only to be disappointed and disillusioned when he could not bring them freedom. About the year 30 C.E., a group of Jews became inspired by a man even though he was quite different from the Messiah they had expected. He was not a soldier, but a rabbi—Rabbi Joshua of the town of Nazareth.

Rabbi Joshua did not believe in warfare, but recommended that the Romans be left to themselves. He did not believe in property, and urged his followers to give their possessions to the poor. In fact, he cared about few things of ordinary life, because he thought ordinary life was coming to an end.

God was going to bring an end to history, Rabbi Joshua told his followers. God would overthrow not only the Romans, but all human rulers. Then God would sit as Judge of all. The righteous would go to heaven and enjoy eternal bliss. The evil would burn in hell forever.

It was consequently foolish to spend one's time thinking about political independence, or property, or family. All that mattered was to prepare one's soul for the "Last Judgment." Rabbi Joshua is reported to have said:

"If anyone slaps you on the right cheek, let him slap your left cheek too. . . . Love your enemies, and pray for those who persecute you, so that you will become the sons of your Father in heaven." [*Matthew 5:39, 44–45*]

A Different Messiah

Apparently Rabbi Joshua had gained enough followers to irritate the Romans. They arrested him and executed him just as they executed other rebels. They nailed him to a cross of wood and left him to die.

Clearly he was not the Messiah that Jews had been expecting. He had not freed the country from Rome. He had not ruled as king. He had not brought peace.

But some of his followers believed in him so strongly that they decided that the mistake must have been theirs. Rabbi Joshua *was* the Messiah, they felt; so *they* must have been wrong in what they had expected the Messiah to be.

So they developed a new concept of "Messiah." They wrote their ideas in Greek so that this new concept could be read by non-Jews.

In Greek, "Joshua the Messiah" was translated "Jesus Christ."

JESUS AND BUDDHA

Jesus was a Jew who believed that humanity would be judged by God's moral laws.

Buddha was a Hindu who cared little for the world, and who was searching for an end to existence.

Yet the similarities between them are startling. Neither claimed to be a god—yet today each is worshipped by millions. Both preached the virtue of poverty—yet each inspired religious organizations that have amassed great wealth. Both were opposed to violence and war—yet much violence has been committed in the name of each. Both were concerned with a speedy end of normal existence—yet each is still worshipped thousands of years after his death.

The concept of Messiah was changed by Christianity. Jesus was pictured, not as an earthly king, but as the ruler of a kingdom in heaven. From a fifteenth-century Russian painting.

A New Definition

The redefining of the term *messiah*, and the belief that Jesus fit that definition, became the foundation of Christianity. What was this new definition which permitted his followers to believe that Jesus was the Messiah—the Christ?

The Jews had been expecting a Messiah who would rule an earthly kingdom. This, said the followers of Jesus, had been the key mistake. The kingdom of the Messiah would not be on earth. It would be in heaven.

Jesus had not brought peace to earth. Again, said his followers, this shows our mistake in thinking so much about earth. In his heavenly kingdom, Jesus would reward the righteous with a life of perfect peace and joy. He could do this because Jesus was not merely the Messiah. He was also the son of God.

If Jesus' kingdom was in heaven, why had he come to earth?

The duty of the Messiah was to bring freedom. "The Jews had been looking for freedom from Rome," said those who believed in Jesus, "but this was wrong. The Messiah has freed us from a heavier burden. He has freed us from sin."

Original Sin

Sin, in this Christian view, was quite different from traditional Jewish concepts. Judaism views sin as our failure to live

THE ROOTS OF ANTI-SEMITISM

The first Christians did not intend to start a new religion. They were Jews. Jesus had been a Jew. They felt that their new ideas completed Judaism, and perfected it. They expected other Jews to come eagerly to their banner.

Most Jews were not interested. Jesus had not fulfilled the ancient expectations of what the Messiah would be. Christians were most successful in attracting Greeks and Romans away from polytheism. Many of these people were tired of their idols. Christianity grew rapidly among them.

Still, Christians were troubled about the Jews. The Jews seemed so stubborn! They refused to worship Jesus. What an insult to the new religion!

The fundamental difference was unbridgeable:

Jews felt that the new ideas of Christianity were unnecessary.
Christians felt the old ideas of Judaism were incomplete.

This basic tension has been behind all Christian forms of anti-Semitism.

A nineteenth-century illustrated Bible depicts the angel Gabriel expelling Adam and Eve from Eden. Christianity views the sin of Adam and Eve as "original sin" which could only be washed away by the sacrifice of the life of Jesus.

up to God's commands in our daily lives. Each person is responsible for his own failings, and for trying to do better. Each Yom Kippur we admit to our sins, pray for forgiveness, and resolve to try to improve in the coming year.

Christians decided that there was another form of sin, a sin no individual could wash away by himself. This was the sin recorded in the story of Adam and Eve, in which the first man and first woman ate the fruit which God had forbidden them.

That *original sin*, said the Christians, had infected all descendants of Adam and Eve—that is, every single human being. Like an incurable disease, it was passed on from generation to generation. *Original sin* became one of the most powerful motor ideas of Christianity.

The only way to cleanse humanity of that supreme sin, Christians said, was a supreme sacrifice. Jesus, the son of God, had given his life on the cross to atone for man's first sin.

Thus in the New Testament—the part of the Christian Bible which tells of Jesus and his early followers, we are told:

God loved the world so much that He gave His only Son, so that everyone who believes in him may not die [when earthly life ends], but have eternal life. [*John 3:16*]

Belief Becomes Crucial

"Everyone who believes in him"—these words are crucial. They show how far Christianity had moved away from Juda-

A fifteenth-century imagining of the "Last Judgment"—that future moment when all people of the earth will be judged by Jesus (who is seated on a heavenly throne). According to Catholic belief, only those people who have accepted the practices of the Catholic Church will achieve "salvation" and be granted entry into heaven. All others will be condemned to never-ending punishment in hell.

While Catholicism believes in one God, like Judaism and Islam, that one God is considered to have a threefold nature—a *Holy Trinity* consisting of God the Father, God the Son, and the Holy Spirit. The Trinity theme shows up frequently in Christian art, as in this sixteenth-century wall painting from a church in Florence, Italy. It shows the Father supporting the Son. Above them is the Holy Spirit, represented by a white bird.

Catholics believe in the doctrine of "virgin birth"—the idea that Jesus' mother, Mary, miraculously remained a virgin even though she gave birth to a son. The image of Madonna and Child—Mary and Jesus—has been a familiar one in much Christian art. Here is a detail of a fifteenth-century painting by the great Italian painter Botticelli.

ism in the century between the birth of Jesus and the time this sentence was written.

Judaism has always been concerned, first and foremost, with *action.* The Torah tells us to obey God's laws. People are judged on the basis of how they do or do not live up to those requirements. Since this judgment can be based on what we actually see, there is no need for us to spend a great deal of time debating those things which no one can prove. Yes, there are discussions about the nature of God and other questions of faith, but there is no standard set of beliefs required of Jews.

Christianity is, on the other hand, a religion focused on saving souls and earning their admittance to the kingdom of heaven. The key to being saved, as the quotation above shows, is *belief.* One must believe that Jesus is the son of God, that he rules the kingdom of heaven, and so on. Proper belief became crucial for Christians.

CATHOLIC SAINTS

All people have the capacity to be good or bad. But a very few people, according to Roman Catholicism, live their lives with such goodness, and with such devotion to the Church, that they become known as *saints*. In almost any Catholic church, statues and paintings of the various saints can be found. They are there to remind Catholics of the goodness of the saints, and to inspire them to follow the saints' example in their own lives.

The Catholic Church has designated many saints throughout its history. Some, like Saint Peter and Saint Paul, lived long ago, and were among the early leaders of Christianity. Other saints lived much closer to our own time. One of the most famous Catholic saints is Saint Francis (left), who was born in Italy over 800 years ago. Francis preached that Christians should live simply, avoiding material possessions and treating everyone with gentleness and humility. His ideas had tremendous influence and attracted many followers. A group that he began, the Franciscan Order of monks, remains to this day one of the most important organizations of the church.

Today, echoes of the name Francis continue to be heard throughout the Catholic world. You can hear it in popular first names like Francis, Franklin, and Francine. The city of San Francisco, founded by Spanish colonizers of the New World, bears a Spanish version of the saint's name.

Building A Church

Since these beliefs were based on what could be neither seen nor proved, someone had to decide what proper belief was.

Priests could decide for the common people. But someone had to be in charge of the priests. The priests of a community were placed under the control of a bishop; bishops were directed by archbishops.

Eventually it was decided that final authority would be given to the bishop of the city of Rome, who was given the special title of Pope.

The Christians hoped to convert everyone to their teachings. Their church, they hoped, would become universal. Another word for universal is *catholic*.

So the organization directed from Rome by the Pope became known as the Roman Catholic Church.

PRIESTS AND RABBIS

A Roman Catholic priest is different in many ways from a Jewish rabbi:

ROMAN CATHOLIC PRIEST	RABBI
May not marry	Normally (and traditionally is encouraged to be) married
Is responsible to Church superiors for his actions and correct teachings	Is responsible to the congregation, but is independent in matters of actions and beliefs
Has special powers to perform the sacraments—the key ceremonies in the life of a Roman Catholic	Although respected for his leadership and knowledge, the rabbi has no special powers
Men only	Women as well as men are now rabbis in non-Orthodox congregations

The Church Triumphant

The Roman Catholic Church became the strongest religious organization in the world. During much of the Middle Ages, all of Europe (except for a small number of Jews) was Catholic. Every little town had its own church and priests. Large cities built great cathedrals. There were large monasteries and convents for men and women who wished to dedicate their lives to the Church by becoming monks and nuns. The Pope was at times the most powerful man in Europe, often richer and more powerful than kings. The popes had their own armies, their own police force, and ruled their own country—a portion of central Italy known as "the Papal States."

The Church Today

That territory was lost to the Church in 1870 when Italy was in the process of becoming a unified country. Today the Pope rules only one-sixth of a square mile—Vatican City, a tiny independent state inside the city of Rome.

Yet by ceasing to compete for territory, the Church gained greater authority over spiritual matters. The Pope is recognized as a leader whose activities attract international attention. Today over 600,000,000 Roman Catholics turn to him for guidance as "the Holy Father."

Michelangelo was one of several architects who worked for over a century to give Rome the largest church of the Christian world. It is called "St. Peter's" after the follower of Jesus who is regarded as the first pope.

Pope John Paul II became the first leader of the Roman Catholic Church to travel the globe. Here he leads an outdoor mass in Poland, before a huge crowd estimated at more than one million people.

HOLY ORDERS

Roman Catholics believe that many ordinary pleasures must be abandoned to lead a truly holy life. Those who wish to dedicate their lives to God enter one of many "Holy Orders" and become known as *monks* and *nuns*. Like priests, monks and nuns do not marry. Some live in secluded *monasteries* and have little to do with the outside world. In some monasteries, members are not even allowed to speak except by special permission from their superiors. By contrast, members of other Holy Orders will devote themselves to service for the outside community, as does this nun working with children in a neighborhood of New York City.

Summary

Jewish followers of Jesus (a Greek translation of the Hebrew name Joshua) believed that he was the Messiah (Christ). His death on the cross proved he was not the earthly king that Jews had been expecting, but his followers believed that Jesus had established the kingdom of heaven. They believed, in addition, that he was the son of God, and had died as a sacrifice to free the world from the sin of Adam and Eve. Priests were placed in charge of determining the right belief about Jesus, with final authority in the bishop of Rome, the Pope. Though the Pope no longer has the authority he had during the Middle Ages, he remains the spiritual leader of 600,000,000 members of the Roman Catholic Church.

CATHOLIC WORSHIP

Roman Catholic worship is centered around rituals called the *sacraments*. Unlike the practices of Judaism, which are really ceremonies designed to remind us of our religion or commandments to help us be better people, the Catholic sacraments are considered essential to gaining salvation. Only Catholic priests have the power to perform these sacraments for their followers.

The sacraments celebrate key moments in a Catholic's life. The first, *Baptism*, comes shortly after birth. With a simple ritual, a baby is considered to be cleansed of original sin and welcomed into the Catholic Church. The priest places a drop of oil on the baby's throat and makes the sign of the cross over him. Shown here is the conclusion of the ritual, when the priest pours water over the baby's head and says, "I baptize you in the name of the Father, the Son, and the Holy Spirit."

At the heart of every important Catholic *mass*, or service, is the sacrament of *Communion*. This is a ritual which recalls the last supper of Jesus. According to the New Testament, Jesus shared wine and bread with his followers, telling them: "This bread is my body, this wine is my blood." During the sacrament of Communion, the priest reenacts these events by offering small wafers and sips of wine to the worshippers. Here a little girl is accompanied by her parents to receive this sacrament for the first time. Her special clothes show that this First Communion is a major event in her life.

As a child grows older he becomes more informed about his religion and is asked to confirm his faith before the congregation. Here a priest and a young man join in the sacrament of *Confirmation*. In an echo of the baptism ceremony, the priest places a drop of oil on the boy's forehead.

Kneeling before the altar in a Mexico City church, a young couple listen as a priest pronounces them "man and wife." Roman Catholicism regards marriage, or *Holy Matrimony*, as a sacrament.

A person may pledge to be good, and yet he sins. The faithful Roman Catholic goes regularly to a priest for the sacrament of *Confession*. The priest listens from behind a grill, as we see here, as the Catholic confesses his sins. Then the priest assigns those prayers or other acts needed to obtain God's forgiveness.

The final sacrament in the life of a Catholic is the *Sacrament of the Sick*, usually given to the elderly and those who are very ill. The priest, in yet another reaffirmation of Baptism, places holy oil on the worshipper's forehead. Because the sacrament is thought to cleanse one of all sins before the moment of death, it often includes Confession and Communion.

13 THE PROTESTANT REVOLUTION

In 1500, the Roman Catholic Church was at the height of its power. It was also at the height of corruption. Leading churchmen were openly ignoring church rules. Although priests were not supposed to marry or have children, many did so anyway. The Pope even used his office to help the careers of his illegitimate children, whom he claimed were nephews and nieces. It was said, "A Pope is someone whom everyone calls 'Father' except his children, who call him 'Uncle.'"

At about this time, a young German suddenly gave up his studies of law in order to become a priest. That act was to lead to the end of the unity of the Roman Catholic Church.

The young priest's name was Martin Luther.

Martin Luther, the founder of Protestantism and the Lutheran Church. Portrait by Luther's friend, Lucas Cranach the Elder.

Martin Luther's Search

Luther was searching for the religious truth that would make him certain of his own salvation. He traveled to Rome, but was horrified at the corruption and immorality of the Church.

Luther decided to find religious truth for himself.

In some ways, this decision proved more important than the conclusions he reached. He was preparing to ignore the organized leadership of the Roman Catholic Church: priests, bishops, cardinals, even the Pope himself. In Luther's eyes, every individual believer was a member of "the universal priesthood of all believers." If a true Christian had the approval of his own conscience, he did not need the approval of the Church.

Much of northern Europe rose in support of him. There was disagreement over what he said, but there was great enthusiasm for his *protest* against Rome. Soon the whole movement became known as "Protestantism."

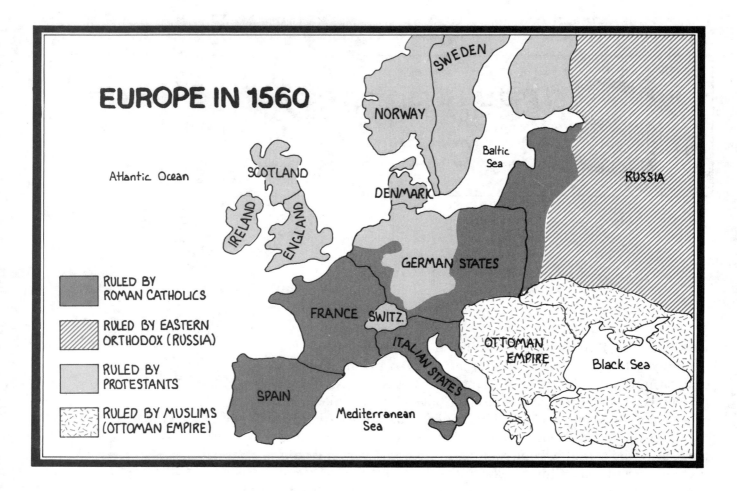

EUROPE IN 1560

Atlantic Ocean

SWEDEN

NORWAY

Baltic Sea

RUSSIA

SCOTLAND

DENMARK

IRELAND

ENGLAND

GERMAN STATES

FRANCE SWITZ.

ITALIAN STATES

SPAIN

OTTOMAN EMPIRE

Black Sea

Mediterranean Sea

RULED BY ROMAN CATHOLICS

RULED BY EASTERN ORTHODOX (RUSSIA)

RULED BY PROTESTANTS

RULED BY MUSLIMS (OTTOMAN EMPIRE)

By 1560, Europe was split between the Roman Catholic and Protestant Churches. England, Scotland, Scandinavia, Switzerland, and most of the German states were ruled by Protestants; the leaders of France, Spain, Italy and most of Eastern Europe remained loyal to the pope.

Luther's Central Idea

What were the ideas that Luther's conscience told him?

Central was the belief that *faith* was the key element in salvation.

While the Roman Catholic Church taught that correct belief was essential, it also stressed the importance of sacraments and *good works*. A person has, in this view, the choice to do good or evil. At the Last Judgment, God will reward the good and punish the evil. We can help ourselves by being good; and by turning to priests for the sacrament of Confession, we can gain God's forgiveness for those sins we confess and truly repent.

Luther rejected this. The Catholic view, he said, implies that God is not in complete control. It seems to say that by choosing a few good deeds and turning to priests for a few good confessions we can influence God to admit us to heaven.

No, said Luther, God decides who will enter heaven for reasons we cannot know or understand. Priests cannot affect this decision. We cannot affect this decision. What we can do is have *faith* that God has chosen *us*. The good works we perform are nothing more than an expression of gratitude for the salvation we believe God has granted us.

A Break Over Communion

Thus Luther attacked a key belief of the Catholic Church. But he went far beyond that. He denied the central mystery of Catholic ritual—the sacrament of Communion.

At every important Roman Catholic mass the priest celebrates the actions performed by Jesus at his last supper. Jesus is said to have blessed bread and wine, passing each to his disciples saying "This is my body" and then "This is my blood." The priest is given the miraculous power to change bread and wine into the body and blood of Jesus.

Of course, the change does not take place in the sense that the bread and wine look or taste like a human body, but the Catholic believes that the *essence* of the substances actually changes. Therefore, in eating the bread and drinking the wine, Catholics believe that they are truly united with Jesus.

Luther believed in a special service with bread and wine, but said the body of Jesus was not *actually* but *spiritually* present. Other Protestant leaders had still different interpretations, and this became a matter of heated debate and even war, but there was basic agreement on an issue of key importance: the Roman Catholic view of Communion was wrong.

The title page of Luther's German Bible, published in 1534.

More Protestant Changes

More and more changes were made. If all people were to be allowed to seek truth in the Bible, the Bible had to be understandable. Luther translated the Bible into German.

It is hard for us to think of this as the revolutionary act it was. Up until that time only a few Catholic priests and schol-

---

RELIGIOUS FREEDOM—FOR <u>ME</u>

While Protestants like Luther believed they had a right to search for the truth, they also believed that there was only one real truth—and that they had found it. They were totally intolerant of others whose search led them in different directions.

Luther was particularly hateful towards the Jews. In his book *Concerning the Jews and their Lies* he urged that the teaching of Judaism be forbidden, and that synagogues be burned.

The Puritans who established colonial Boston were searching for religious freedom—for themselves. When a young preacher named Roger Williams disagreed with them, he was banished from the colony. Williams left and founded Providence, Rhode Island, where he became the first American to work for complete religious toleration.

ars knew Latin, the language of the only available version of the Christian Bible. This gave them a special kind of power, as they could give an official interpretation of scripture to the common people.

A translation meant that commoners could read and interpret the Bible for themselves. This concept was so objectionable to the established church that a friend of Luther, William Tyndale, was burned at the stake for translating the Bible into English.

A New View of Priests

Luther had completely changed the Christian view of what a priest should be. The Catholic priest hears Confession and gives pardon for sins. He has the power to perform the miracle of Communion. He was, in Luther's time, the source of knowledge of scripture. Given these special powers, he was to dedicate his whole life to God. The Catholic priest can never marry.

Having rejected all the special powers of priesthood, Luther also rejected the special restrictions on priestly life. He favored marriage for priests, and set an example by marrying a former nun and raising six children.

Hundreds of Religions

For more than 1,000 years, the Roman Catholic Church had insisted that its officials were the only ones who could determine true belief. The Church had created armies to enforce this principle. A police force, the Inquisition, was given the power to judge and execute anyone found guilty of false belief.

The Church feared that if any person could decide what is true, almost any new belief could be used to create a new religious sect.

The Protestant Revolution proved that there was justification for this fear. Once Luther had shown that a person could be Christian and still hold beliefs of which Rome did not approve, many people developed their own ideas. For a few years there was only one Protestant religion. Soon there were several denominations, then a dozen, then dozens more.

Protestantism Today

Today there are hundreds of Protestant denominations—enough to cover almost every shade of belief about the life and death of Jesus. The churches behave very differently.

Some Protestant churches, such as Episcopalians and Lutherans, have bishops and a strict church organization. Other

After Luther came other leaders whose teachings led to the formation of new Protestant churches. John Calvin (1509–1564) led the Reformation in Geneva, Switzerland. He favored a much more drastic break with the practices of Roman Catholicism. He also preached that a church should be run by the people who belong to it, not by a pope or bishops or priests. His ideas spread to England and Scotland, where his followers became known as Presbyterians, and eventually to America. Today the Presbyterian Church is one of the largest Protestant groups in America.

CHRISTIANITY AND THE JEWISH BIBLE

The Jewish Bible consists of thirty-six Hebrew books, which tell much of the early history of Judaism, contain many stories and poems, and report the actual words of the prophets of Israel.

Christians believe that the life and death of Jesus began a new *covenant* (contract) between humanity and God, replacing the earlier covenant made at Mount Sinai with the Jewish people. They accept the Hebrew books as holy but do not consider them to be the complete record of God's word. Their Bible also includes the Greek books which tell of Jesus and his followers, and which include letters written by Saint Paul and other early teachers of Christianity. These books are called the *New Testament*, because they deal with the "new covenant." The Christian name for the Jewish Bible is *Old Testament*, or "old covenant." Because the word "old" is used in the sense of "outdated," Jews do not accept or use this term.

Another Protestant group influenced by Calvin, the Puritans, founded the English colonies of Massachusetts and Connecticut. The Salem Witch Trials, conducted by Puritan leaders in the 1690's, were an extreme example of the intolerance often shown in the early days of Protestantism.

Protestant groups have no bishops, and each church conducts its affairs as its members wish.

In some Protestant churches, the priests wear special elaborate clothes in services (as Catholics do). Others, like the Baptists, wear everyday suits.

Some churches have fought religious wars. The Quakers, however, do not believe that it is ever right to strike or hurt any other human being.

While Luther approved of marriage, even for priests, the Shakers did not approve of marriage—for anyone. Their church has virtually disappeared, since the Shakers could have no children.

Most Protestants believe in Jesus as the Son of God. But many Unitarians feel that he was only an inspired teacher. As a result, some Unitarians no longer consider themselves Christians at all.

A baptism in the Jordan River, in Israel—the same river where, according to the New Testament, Jesus was baptized. The Baptists, who make up the largest Protestant group in America, believe that Baptism should be reserved for adults (unlike Roman Catholics, who perform Baptism within a few days of birth). They base this practice not only on the tradition that Jesus was baptized as an adult, but also on the idea that an adult can make a conscious decision to accept Christianity, while a baby has no choice in the matter.

Anglican choir boys sing Christmas carols at Winchester Cathedral. The Anglican Church—also known as the Church of England—was created by King Henry VIII. It is still the dominant religion of England. In America, the Anglican Church developed its own leadership and became known as the Episcopal Church. While they are two separate organizations, the Anglicans and Episcopalians remain very similar in beliefs and practices.

In the United States, where Protestantism is the dominant religion, there are hundreds of different churches competing for followers. The six largest American Protestant denominations are the Baptists, Methodists, Lutherans, Presbyterians, Episcopalians, and Congregationalists. How many can you find listed here?

The Success of Christianity

The unified church of the Middle Ages, in which one man ruled all the Christians of Europe, is gone forever.

The result, however, is that a very wide range of beliefs can find a home within the Christian world. There are approximately 435,000,000 non-Catholic Christians. This means the total Christian population is over one billion, making it the largest religious group in the world.

Summary

Martin Luther's protests against the Catholicism of the 1500's split the Church. Luther taught that faith, not good works,

NOT CATHOLIC, NOT PROTESTANT

There are Christian groups who are neither Catholic nor Protestant. The Eastern Orthodox Churches, which originated in the eastern part of the Roman Empire and spread throughout eastern Europe, broke from the Catholic Church in 1054 because they refused to accept the authority of the Pope in Rome. Their beliefs are much like Catholicism, but they have their own national churches and leaders. They also maintain a strong presence in the Middle East. (Above right) The Greek Orthodox Monastery of St. Catherine is located at the traditional site of Mount Sinai in the Sinai desert.

The Church of Jesus Christ of Latter-Day Saints, whose followers are usually known as the "Mormons," began in the first half of the nineteenth century. The Mormon prophet was a New Englander named Joseph Smith, who claimed to receive a direct communication from heaven about the true Christian Church in the New World. Under the leadership of Smith, and later Brigham Young, the Mormons gained numbers, resisted persecution, and gradually moved westward until they established themselves in the territory of Utah. There they founded Salt Lake City and built their famous temple (right). Nearby is the world headquarters of the Mormon church, which today is a powerful organization actively seeking converts all over the world.

was the key element in salvation. He denied the Catholic understanding of Communion. He translated the Bible into German so that it could be widely read. By establishing the principle that individuals (rather than a Church) could determine religious belief, he set off the Protestant movement, which eventually gave rise to hundreds of different denominations. The wide variety of Christian religions has about a billion followers.

THE CHRISTIAN YEAR

"Joy to the world, the Lord is come, let earth receive her king." So begins the famous Christmas carol which reflects the joy Christians find in a personal relationship with their heavenly king. The life of Jesus has inspired some of the world's greatest artists, while the celebrations of events in Jesus' life are the key moments in the Christian calendar.

In the birth of Jesus, the Christian sees the miracle of the "Virgin Birth"—God becoming man, born to the Virgin Mary. (Above) In the painting by sixteenth-century Dutch artist Gerard David, Mary and her husband Joseph join with earthly shepherds and angels from heaven in adoration of the child Jesus. This miracle is celebrated each year as the holiday of Christmas. (Right) The faithful assemble to observe Christmas in Bethlehem, the town just south of Jerusalem where Jesus was born.

After three years of preaching in the Galilee, Jesus traveled south to Jerusalem to celebrate Passover. According to the New Testament, he had developed such a following that his arrival in the city became a triumphant procession, where the people "took branches of palm trees and went out to meet him." This seventeenth-century Russian painting (right) recreates that scene. Today, Christians carry palm leaves on Palm Sunday to recall this event.

(Above) An engraving based on a famous painting by Leonardo da Vinci shows Jesus and his followers at the Last Supper (a Passover seder). Later that same night one of his followers betrayed Jesus to the Romans. He was captured and the next day, known as Good Friday, he was crucified. (Below) Christians observe Good Friday in Jerusalem, reeanacting Jesus' forced march to execution.

After his arrest and crucifixion, Jesus was taken from the cross and buried in a tomb. But within a few days the tomb was found to be empty. His followers believed he had been resurrected (raised from the dead) and gone to his throne in heaven. Enflamed with the conviction that they had experienced a miracle, they set out to bring their news to the world. The engraving (above) by the German artist Dürer, shows Jesus rising from his tomb before Roman soldiers. The high point of the Christian year is the holiday of Easter, which celebrates the resurrection of Jesus. (Below) Easter mass at the Church of the Holy Sepulchre in Jerusalem, traditionally held to be the site of the resurrection.

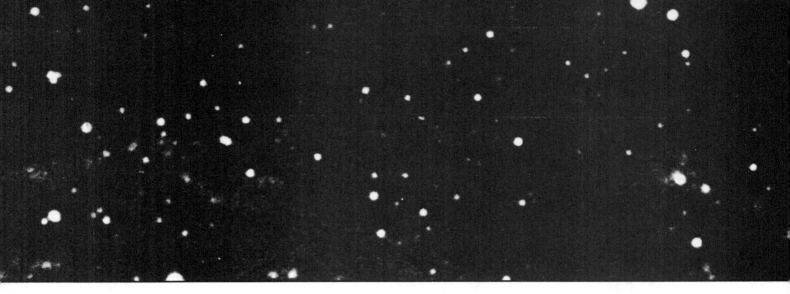

PART FIVE
CHALLENGES TO RELIGION

14 BELIEFS IN CONFLICT

Mark Twain gained world-wide fame by writing *Tom Sawyer* and *Huckleberry Finn*. One day he picked up a newspaper and was astounded by what he read. The paper reported that Mark Twain had just died! A reporter came for further details and was amazed to be met by the author himself. Mark Twain commented wryly: "The reports of my death are greatly exaggerated."

Much more recently, *Time Magazine* ran a cover story concerning the view that some people have taken of religion. The controversial cover read, "God is Dead."

If shown that magazine cover, a heavenly observer might smile and, like Mark Twain, say that the report of God's death was "greatly exaggerated." Religious organizations around the world have been growing—some at astounding rates.

Changing Solutions

In the years between 1945 (the end of the Second World War) and 1980, there was an enormous growth in America of synagogues and churches. Many of these were Reform and Conservative synagogues and similar modern-thinking churches, which appealed to the young, adventurous families who were creating new communities in the suburbs of major cities. These religions offered new challenges and choices to those whose lives had similar challenges and choices during the exciting post-war years.

During the 1980's, the fastest growing religious organizations were those which offered the simplest solutions to the problems of the world. This is perhaps not surprising. The world was becoming a more difficult place to understand. In 1945, America was the unquestioned leader of the world, filled with prosperity and standing alone among world powers with the atom bomb. By the 1980's many nations had atomic weapons, and Japan, a defeated nation after the Second World War,

The adventurous architecture of this synagogue reflects the adventurous spirit of those who created new suburban communities after the Second World War. Pictured is Congregation B'nai Israel in Woonsocket, Rhode Island.

was flooding our shores with automobiles and electronic products.

The Appeal of Simplicity

Our world is changing so quickly that any of us would welcome something simple and definite that we could hang onto with confidence.

Most of us, however, feel that as the world becomes increasingly complex, solutions to problems will become more complex.

The most traditional, orthodox, and fundamentalist religions disagree. They feel that worrying about complexity is a mistake. Each of these religions offers a precise, definite, statement of absolute truth about God, salvation, or the Messiah. The fundamentalist groups—those which claim that their holy scriptures are literally and exactly true—have the additional appeal of providing an "answer book" with the "perfect truth." (There are also groups called "cults" which imitate religions and offer very definite—and very dangerous—answers to human problems. We will examine these false religions in the next chapter.)

Dangerous Devotion

Any religion which gives satisfaction to its followers and brings no harm to others is, in some ways, to be admired.

Unfortunately, many deep-felt beliefs are far from harmless. They often lead to violent disagreements between believers and non-believers. In 1979, Muslim fanatics took control of Iran and ruthlessly executed their opponents. They rooted out many modern developments in the country, and worked to return women to the second-class status which is traditional for them in the Muslim world.

Religious clashes are by no means limited to old-fashioned groups who wish to turn the clock back to another era. Catholics and Protestants have a long-standing war in Northern Ireland. Christians and Muslims battle in Lebanon. And in India, Prime Minister Indira Gandhi, a Hindu, sent an army into the holy temple of a religious minority, the Sikhs. Shortly afterwards, a Sikh assassinated the Prime Minister.

Problems of Education

Religious differences can create problems which are less bloody, but are still very serious. For example, how are we to teach science? How should American schools explain the creation of the world?

Every reputable scientist states that the earth was created over billions of years. They have evidence of every kind—except the evidence of the Bible. The Bible states that the earth was created in six days, and some large and powerful Chris-

A fundamentalist preacher leads his followers in prayer. The Bible in his upraised hand, and the strong emotion evident on his face, seem to emphasize the simple claim of Christian fundamentalism: "All truth is in the Bible."

Muslim fundamentalism, which is now in control of Iran and gaining strength throughout the Middle East, is so opposed to the modern world it will even dictate what kind of clothing people wear. Women have been forced to return to the traditional Muslim dress which covers most of the body—even the face.

Two of America's most famous lawyers—Clarence Darrow (left) and William Jennings Bryan—opposed each other at the "Scopes monkey trial" of 1925. A Tennessee biology teacher, John Scopes, was tried and found guilty of teaching evolution in the public schools. Today, over fifty years later, many fundamentalists are still opposed to the teaching of evolution in the public school systems of America.

tian fundamentalist groups believe that this is literally true—six calendar days. They therefore insist that schools teach—as an alternative scientific theory—the Biblical story.

Does a group have a right to have its religious beliefs taught as science?

Birth Control

Equally difficult is the question of birth control. The Roman Catholic Church teaches that nothing must interfere with the possibility of a married couple having a child. In addition, a woman who becomes pregnant must not do anything to prevent her child from being born. To interfere with the creation of a new life is, in the eyes of the Catholic Church, little different from committing murder.

Others—including most Reform and Conservative Jews—feel quite the opposite. The birth of a wanted baby into a family which can care for and love it is indeed one of life's miracles. But many babies are not wanted. In some countries, high birth rates lead to overpopulation and starvation. Because of this, many feel that new life should be brought into the world only when parents truly want a child. A woman should become a mother by choice, not by chance.

There is an ongoing struggle in the United States and elsewhere between these opposing views.

Questions concerning birth control and abortion arouse strong emotional reactions on both sides of the issues.

Why Bother?

One response to all this would be to say, "Why bother? If no one religion has found all the answers, why should I get involved with *any* of them?"

In former ages, a person *had* to be a member of one religion or another. Society was organized around religions. One could hardly live, or die and be buried, without the help of some sort of religious organization.

This is no longer the case. It is perfectly possible to live a full and happy life ignoring the world of religion. The secular (non-religious) world has much to offer in the way of attractions, interest, and entertainment. Science tells us a great deal about the universe. Why ask for anything more?

Science has given us weapons of enormous power—even the power to destory civilization. It tells us very little about what is worth fighting for.

Some Answers

One answer is that religious experiences can be delightful and fun and inspiring. There is nothing in the secular world, for example, that replaces the joy of a family coming together for a Passover Seder to celebrate the 3,000-year-old victory of Moses in his struggle to free an enslaved people.

There is a more basic and more important answer, however. The secular world is not equipped to answer our most basic and critical questions.

Science can teach us a great deal about what the world is like, and how it works, but it does not tell us why the world was created, or suggest whether our life on earth really matters.

Science can often tell us how to preserve life or how to end life, but it is neutral as to which course we should take. Scientists created the machines which the Nazis used to send millions of innocent people to their deaths. Pure science tells us nothing of whether the Nazis were right or wrong.

It gives us no more guidance on the personal level. Science can tell us long before a baby is born many things about what the child will be like. It does not tell a pregnant woman what she should do if her baby will be born with a serious birth defect. Should she have the baby? Or should she ask doctors to end her pregnancy?

Religions try to deal with questions such as these. Of course, different religions disagree as to what the answers should be. To be more accurate: these questions are so difficult that people cannot agree on one answer to them, and religions reflect those different views.

Where there is freedom of religion, as in America, individuals may join any church or synagogue where the answers suggested seem to be true and meaningful.

Summary

There has been a great growth of religious institutions in recent years, though different types of beliefs have had popularity at different periods. Sometimes the commitments of various groups have brought them into conflict. This is in part because religions deal with the very difficult questions and choices in life for which there are no simple solutions and which scientific analysis cannot answer. Where there is freedom of religion, people are free to search for answers that they find personally meaningful.

15 IS THERE A GOD?

In the past chapters, we have seen many different ideas about God, and what makes life meaningful.

Do you remember our image in Chapter 2? We spoke of many people looking at a light, but each looking through a different-colored glass. Each sees the light differently.

But all agreed that there is a light.

There are people, however, who see no light at all. They say, "You religious people worry about what God wants. This worrying is pointless. There is no God."

A person who says there is no God is called an *atheist*. (This comes from two Greek roots: *a*—"without" and *theos*—"god.")

The religious person observes the universe and says, "How wonderful is God's universe!" The athiest says, "The universe is huge, and we are alone in a tiny corner of it."

Deciding What Is Right

Actually, a great many people who talk about being atheists haven't really thought a great deal about what the term implies. You probably know people who talk about atheism, but are really saying, "I don't have to go to religious school. I'll just be a good person. That's logical. I don't have to worry about all this 'God' stuff that no one can prove."

This sounds impressive. But is that position really so logical? How does this sort of atheist decide how to be a good person?

"That's no problem," says the atheist. "We may have differences of opinion on some details, but the basics are simple. For example, we can all say that murder is evil."

"Wait a minute," says the religious person. "That's cheating. You've denied religion, but now you take your principle from the Bible: 'You shall not murder.' Once you leave out religion, I am free to listen to totally different views: Hitler's, for example. He taught that murder was good, as long as the murder was of the millions of people he said were inferior."

"Just because there is a good idea in the Bible," says the atheist, "doesn't mean we have to rely on the Bible to believe it. 'You shall not steal' may be in the Bible, but obviously we shouldn't steal. If everyone steals from everyone else, the whole world would be in chaos."

"Why should an atheist worry about the whole world?" says the religious person. "I have that concern because I believe God rules the universe and has, through Jews, given the world a set of laws to help people live with respect and caring for one another. If I didn't think that—if I didn't believe that stealing was *really* wrong according to a religiously developed stand-

---

WITHOUT GOD, "THE END ALWAYS JUSTIFIES THE MEANS"

Niccolo Machiavelli lived in Italy in 1500, and wrote a book telling how to be the perfect ruler. The book, *The Prince*, says that for the ruler good and evil means what works for him—"the end justifies the means." Some of his other sayings:

"A wise ruler ought not to keep his word when by doing so it would be against his interest. If men were all good, this principle would not be a good one; but as they are bad, and would not keep their word to you, so you are not bound to keep your word to them."

"It is well to seem merciful, faithful, humane, sincere, religious, and also to be so; but you must be prepared when necessary to change to the opposite qualities."

Accepting the moral teachings of the Bible while denying the existence of God is something like saying: "I accept all the products of science, but I just don't believe in the scientific method."

ard based on centuries of belief in God's law—I would certainly feel free to do whatever seemed best for *me*."

Some Agreement

The debate goes on like this. The atheist wants to deny the existence of God, which cannot be proved, and yet keep his belief in right and wrong. He has no basis on which to justify that belief, however, except his own feelings of what makes sense. Another person may have totally different feelings.

The religious person says there is a real standard of right and wrong by which actions can be measured. Murder is *wrong*—not just cruel. Stealing is *wrong*—not just selfish.

Belief in a real measure by which we judge right and wrong is at least the beginning of what religion is about.

So people who are committed to the moral code brought to the world in the Bible, even if they deny the existence of God, cannot be true atheists. They may disagree with many of the teachings of organized religion, but they accept its most important principle—that there is a real standard of right and wrong. They may argue many points with the religious person over ways of seeing "the light"—but they still agree that the light is truly there.

The Position of the Atheist

The atheist sees that different religions have very different beliefs and takes this as proof that "the light is just an illusion."

The religious person sees that most people in the world believe in God, and takes this as proof that "the light is there." The atheist says firmly, "No. If there were a God, surely God would do a better job of letting people know what is expected of them."

The atheist examines history books and reads the daily newspapers, and sees that some people who have claimed to be very religious have done terrible things. "If there is a God," says the atheist, "why are people who claim to be religious allowed to commit murders and massacres?"

The atheist looks at the world and sees that all too often good people suffer and bad people go unpunished. A religious person may insist that each will be rewarded or punished after death, but the atheist sees no evidence for this. "Let's look at facts," he says. "There is no evidence for life-after-death, but there is lots of evidence that good people suffer in *this* life. If there is a God, then God ought to be able to deal with *this* life justly."

Problems of Atheism

These arguments are powerful as far as they go, but they omit important facts.

If the great religious leaders of the world have failed to agree on one image of God, or one picture of the universe, they have still shown themselves to be inspired and inspiring. They thrilled many of those who knew them. They revolutionized human thought. They set ideals which billions of people feel are the highest goals of humanity, and have been admired by the vast majority of the most intelligent people who ever lived.

The atheist must explain how all this was possible if these leaders were speaking nonsense.

What are the Rewards?

We cannot explain why good people sometimes suffer and bad people sometimes win. But we do know that it only makes sense to talk about "being good" when we do not know the result. We are not "being good" to take care of a dog if someone pays us to do it. It's just good business! But when we would rather go to a movie or play with our friends, and we don't even know if someone will thank us, and we still care for the dog because he needs us, then we are truly being good.

Some of the great triumphs of the human spirit come about when people have done what is right even though they knew the results would be unrewarding, dangerous, or even fatal. It is true that some people who claimed to be religious have been

Sometimes good people suffer and bad people go unpunished. Why should God allow this? People have been asking that question for thousands of years—it is even found in the Bible, in the Book of Job. No one has a perfect answer.

Rabbi Abraham Joshua Heschel (second from right) is joined by (from left) the Reverend Ralph Abernathy, the Reverend Martin Luther King, Jr., and Ralph Bunche at a 1965 freedom march in Selma, Alabama. During the Civil Rights movement, religious leaders linked arms to gain equal rights for all American citizens, regardless of race. This was a righteous act because they did not know what the outcome would be. Some people were hurt and even killed—but eventually new laws were passed outlawing racial discrimination.

brutal and savage butchers. But the religions of the world have also produced many of humanity's most admired heroes and saints. Atheism has not had a distinctive record of producing admirable people, but has helped create such tyrants as Hitler and the dictators of Russia and China.

Yet in those sentences we slipped back into using terms the atheist cannot accept: saints, admirable people, heroes. Such terms imply a standard of good and evil by which human actions can be judged.

And when we say that there is a standard, we are really saying: "There is a light."

Summary

Atheism is the belief that there is no God. Many people who use the term have not thought it out fully. They want to do away with many of the aspects of organized religion, but keep its moral principles. This is not a position that can be defended logically. Most of the world's people can agree that there is a standard of right and wrong. That this standard exists is one of the most important principles of religion.

16 THE EVIL OF CULTS

People who believe in a religion often try to convince others of the truth of their beliefs.

Some religions set strict rules for their worshippers to obey.

Every religion needs financial support from its followers.

But there are a growing number of organizations which pretend to be religious, which take total control of their members, and which use the money of the members to make the "church" leaders rich.

These groups are known as *cults*.

What Do Cults Offer?

Cults offer the simplest possible solution to problems: Forget them, and place your confidence in the cult's leader, who is the source of all truth.

In the cult, all decisions are made by the leaders. Members are told where to live, what to eat, how to work and whom to marry. Their money is put in the care of the cult.

All this is done in the name of wonderful ideals. The group claims to help society. The group claims to free people from the evils of the world. The group may identify itself as the only one which will survive God's final judgment.

What Do Cults Really Do?

Unfortunately, cults are not at all what they claim to be. They do not improve society or help the poor. They use the money they raise to make the cult and its leaders rich.

They force cult members to work long hours for little or no pay, frequently under terrible conditions. Sometimes the cults are involved in violence.

Women are made to do lowly tasks while a few men make the decisions which control their lives.

Children may be neglected and beaten, or they may be forced

Korean cult leader Sun Myung Moon, top center, performs a marriage ceremony for more than 2,000 couples. The partners have been assigned to each other by Moon's Unification Church.

to obey strict rules. Some rules may be ridiculous (such as not eating onions), but others are designed to keep children separated from others their own age who are not cult members. They may be forbidden television and sports. They may be forced to wear odd clothing, weird hairstyles, or to shave their heads. Ordinary kids are said to be "children of Satan"—wicked and contaminating.

In some cults, children are taken away from their parents and sent to special schools. They are trained to be loyal only to the cult leader, and hardly know their parents at all.

Why Join Such a Group?

Why would anyone join such an organization?

This is an excellent question. Few people would join this kind of group if they knew what they were getting into.

Yet people do join cults, precisely because they do *not* know what the cults are really like. This is not accidental. The cults feel free to lie or trick or cheat in order to get what they want. They do not feel this lying is wrong if it is done for the good of the cult.

These young people have given up their homes and families to chant "Hare Krishna" in honor of the Hindu god Krishna—and ask for money for their cult, Krishna Consciousness.

How Does It Happen?

The victim is often a student of college age. Perhaps he or she is a freshman, away from home for the first time, trying to adjust to a totally new situation. Or perhaps the student is a senior, worried about finding a job and a new life after graduation.

Another student appears and makes friends. "You are a great person," says the cult member. "I have some terrific friends who would just love to meet you. Why don't you come and have dinner with us?"

The victim becomes the guest of honor among seven or eight young people who listen to him with fascination, telling him how wonderful and interesting he is. They just can't get enough of him. When the evening is over, they beg him to join them for a weekend retreat. "You'd fit in so well. Besides, it's free."

QUOTES FROM CULT LEADERS

Here are some selected quotes from leaders of cults, taken from *Science Digest*, January 1982.

Because your mind troubles you, give it to me. It won't trouble me. (Guru Maharaj J., *Divine Light Mission*)

A very effective thought-control technique could also be worked out from Scientology, which could be used to make individuals into willing slaves. (L. Ron Hubbard, *Church of Scientology*)

I am your brain. (Rev. Sun Myung Moon, *Unification Church*)

Brainwashing

The weekend turns out to be filled with lectures—with no questions permitted. The victim is never left alone. He gets little sleep. Everyone seems to be aware of some "higher truth" but never quite says what it is. There is repetition, monotony, a form of hypnosis all mixed with physical exhaustion.

As you read the last paragraph, you may have thought a weekend like that sounds boring and stupid. In practice, it is the highly effective technique of brainwashing. By the end of just one weekend, the victim is no longer in complete control of himself.

Members of the group follow the victim and "bomb him with love," saying how much they want him to be part of their group. They offer no ordinary group membership, however. The victim must break his family ties, and give himself totally to his "new family."

Under this kind of pressure, minds do snap. The victim joins. He may still not be able to think clearly enough to realize he has joined a cult.

Empty Minds—and Empty Pockets

The cult takes over the ability of the victim to think. All decisions are made for him. The leader of the group is said to be all-knowing. He may be described as the Messiah, or even as God. His orders are supreme—no one is to question or even think about any orders he may give. You serve him with your work and, if necessary, your life.

And you most definitely serve him with your money. You give all your property to the cult. You may live in poverty while the leader and his henchmen enjoy luxury. One such leader had mansions all over the world. Another wore a dozen large diamonds. A third had 85 imported automobiles! You aren't to worry about this. You are helping to glorify your miraculous teacher.

The Difficulty of Escape

It is far from easy to escape from a cult once you have been sucked into it. Your money is taken from you. You are shut off from your family, and from news of the outside world. You may be threatened with violence or death if you "betray" the group by leaving it.

There are people who do escape, but often they have a very difficult time adjusting to the real world. Learning again how to think for yourself and make personal decisions is not easy after you have gone through a period of brainwashing.

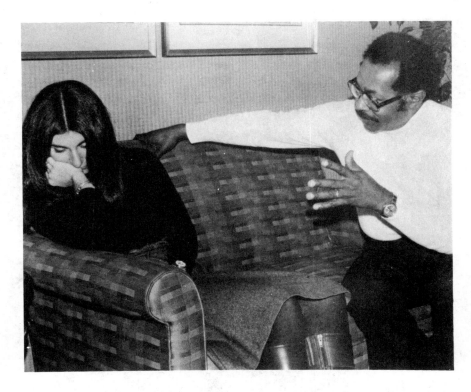

This girl has been taken out of her cult, and is working with the man at right to be "deprogrammed." She has far to go before she can regain use of her mind and the ability to communicate.

It is particularly difficult to admit that there are no simple solutions to the problems of the world.

Some people never do recover their minds.

Limitless Evil

No one knows the exact number of functioning cults. While there are cults which seek publicity, others remain small and secretive. One thing is certain: there are a great many of them. The best guess is that there are between 1,000 and 3,000 cults in the United States, with memberships totaling between two and three million.

They prove what can happen when the idea of religion is corrupted by dictatorial leaders. The great tragedy is that the victims most easily deceived are intelligent young people, well-to-do (the cults aren't interested in victims who have no money to contribute), with high ideals. They are attracted by the promise of warm friendship among concerned people who want to improve the world.

In fact, there seems to be no limit to the evil that cults can do. One crazed cult leader took his followers to South America, promising to create a paradise for them. When his plans did not work out, he ordered his people to commit suicide.

At his command, the men, women, and children lined up to drink Kool-Aid mixed with deadly poison. There in the jungle, 900 cult members suffered a meaningless death.

Jonestown, Guyana (South America), November 1978. Around a vat containing a cyanide drink are bodies of some of the 913 people driven to mass suicide by an insane cult leader. There seems to be no limit to the evils of cults.

Summary

Organizations which imitate the forms of religion, but which ask members to give blind obedience to a dictatorial leader, are called "cults." While claiming to pursue high ideals, they actually brainwash their members, forcing them to break ties with their families, making them work long hours under dreadful conditions, and taking their money. In an extreme example of the evils of these groups, an entire cult was led to group suicide.

17 THE MELTING POT

Religious groups used to live quite separate from each other. The great centers of Buddhism were divided from the Hindus of India by huge mountains and broad seas. The Christian world had little communication with the Muslim world. Jews who lived among Christians or Muslims were often shut away in ghettos.

There was also no great distinction between the religious world and the secular world. Often life centered around religion. Religious institutions provided education, health services, and charity. Impressive religious observances might be a community's most exciting entertainment.

Today all this has changed. Mighty mountains and vast seas are no obstacle to jet planes. Satellites bring television programming to tiny towns in remote regions. Schools, colleges, business, immigration, and tourism bring together all nationalities, races, and religions.

Good or Bad?

In many areas of life, we think of the mixing of cultures as a good thing. It is good for us to be able to read books and see movies that have been created in other countries. It is good for us to travel and see how others live.

For Jews, it has been particularly wonderful to have been welcomed to America. Most of us are the descendants of people who came here about a century ago. Within only a few years, our grandparents or great-grandparents became an accepted part of the American scene, able to enjoy the rights and opportunities of the world's leading democracy.

But mixing of cultures can also have its unfortunate side. Valuable parts of one culture may disappear as the smaller group mixes into the larger. Its language, its customs, and its literature may be lost.

Thousands of new immigrants, most from Cuba, gather in a large naturalization ceremony at Miami's Orange Bowl to proclaim their joy in their newly acquired American citizenship. Many nationalities have come to the United States. Each tries to preserve its own heritage while enjoying the benefits of the total American scene.

The process of one group being absorbed into another is called *assimilation*.

Making Choices

The culture of the smaller group may not be completely lost. Parts of it may be added to the general culture. The most obvious example is food. We can go to a supermarket and choose from delicious items brought to America by immigrants from many lands. We can have Italian pizza one night, Jewish matzoh ball soup another, and Chinese chow mein the third.

In America, we are blessed with freedom of religion. All religions mentioned in this book, and a great many more, are observed in the United States. Whatever our religious preference, we may follow it in our way.

Choices do have to be made, however, when the mixing of cultures means the meeting of young people of different religions. Some will fall in love and marry.

Marriage between members of different groups is called *intermarriage*.

Obstacles

Religion does not work the way a supermarket does. We cannot pray facing Jerusalem on Monday and Mecca on Tuesday, believe that Jesus was the son of God on Wednesday and that there is no God on Thursday.

As we have seen, different religions teach very different things. They give very different views of how we should look at the world, and how we should live our lives.

Conversion

When people of different religions fall in love, one may take on the religion of the other. There is a ceremony of *conversion* in which a person officially accepts a new religion. (One can, of course, convert to a new religion because of personal belief,

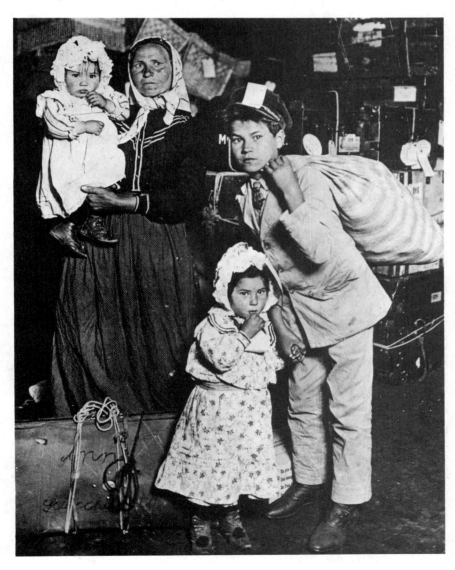

This woman, or her children, were fully accepted as part of America's culture. But how much may also have been lost by this process of assimilation?

with no immediate plans to marry a member of that religion.)

A marriage between a person born into a religion and a person converted into a religion is not really intermarriage at all. Both wife and husband have become members of the same religion.

This can work out in interesting ways. Frequently the convert, having accepted a religion by choice, sees exciting things that those born into the faith have taken for granted. Many converts to Judaism have become synagogue leaders.

Problems of Intermarriage

Marriages between people who preserve separate religions present special concerns. Any marriage involves two people adjusting to the differences between them. Differences in religion can make that more difficult.

Jews and Christians who marry sometimes are surprised at

A group of "Jews for Jesus" stage a demonstration in New York City. Various cults and cult-like groups are specifically directed at converting Jews to Christianity.

how much they do *not* share. "He really believes that Jesus was the son of God!" "She gets too upset when there is a movie about the Nazis." "His family just isn't like mine." "They're all so worried about the State of Israel."

And there are often arguments over how children are to be raised.

Avoiding a Decision

What are children to be taught by parents who do not agree about religion?

The least satisfactory answer is to say, "We'll let them learn about many religions. When they are adults, they can decide for themselves."

There are many good reasons for learning about the religions of the world. (That's why this book was written!) And every person should be able to decide what religion he or she wants to practice.

But that is not the same as saying that children should receive no guidance from their parents.

No parents would say, "Many people think that brushing your teeth is a good idea, but we don't want to force our opinions on our children. We'll let them brush or not brush according to their moods. When they are adults, they can decide whether or not to keep on brushing."

Children are entitled to guidance in keeping healthy teeth. They are also entitled to guidance with something that affects our most basic views of the world, such as religion.

One or the Other

Sometimes parents can agree that children will be brought up in the faith of either the mother or the father. It has been possible to have happy homes where this choice was made. For example, a father may remain Christian while his children grow up Jewish. He may actively participate in Jewish activities and celebrations with his wife and children while personally keeping the traditions of his own parents.

But what does it mean to have a Christian father participating in his Jewish son's Bar Mitzvah? Many rabbis and congregations will not permit this. The non-Jewish parent and family attend and share the joy of the occasion, but are not given privileges reserved to Jews such as reading the service and reciting the blessings over the Torah.

One way or another, some difficult choices have to be made. This is a fact which intermarried parents must be prepared to face.

Jews are a tiny minority of the world's population. Every one of us is an important member of the Jewish people; every one of us has a role to play in learning about Judaism and keeping its message alive.

Assimilation and Judaism

Assimilation in all its forms is of concern to Jews.

On the one hand, we want to be an accepted part of the society in which we live. Having been shut away in ghettos for many generations, we now want to be involved in all possible activities. The modern world has marvelous opportunities to offer, and we want to enjoy them.

On the other hand, we have cultural treasures which are hard to preserve in the midst of a great non-Jewish society. We have Jewish languages—Hebrew and Yiddish—but few opportunities to use them even if we study them. We have Jewish holidays, but they often interfere with our secular schedules. We have fine works of Jewish literature, but enjoying them may take more effort than seeing the latest movie or television program.

Intermarriage is of special concern to us. We are a tiny minority—some 17 million world-wide. Because Adolf Hitler slaughtered one-third of all living Jews, there are still fewer of us today than there were when he came to power in 1933. And children of intermarriages are statistically less likely to grow up to be committed Jews than are children of all-Jewish families.

Each Jewish person—each Jewish family—is valuable in preserving the world of Judaism, and passing it on to the people of the future.

The Key Question

But this brings us back to our key question—the very question with which this book began.

Is Judaism special?

Does it matter to the world if Judaism survives?

It is time that we go back to that question, and try to give it an answer.

Summary

The mixing of one culture into another is called "assimilation." There are positive sides to it, but problems as well, such as the loss of cultural identity by the smaller group. Jews, being a tiny minority, are concerned about losing our people through assimilation and intermarriage. But this raises the question posed at the beginning of the book: Does it matter if Judaism survives?

PART SIX
REACHING A CONCLUSION

18 WHAT MAKES JUDAISM SPECIAL?

A photograph in a newspaper is printed with thousands of tiny dots of ink. If you look at it with a powerful magnifying glass you will see the dots—but you will not be able to see the picture! Only if you give up seeing every detail can you see the picture as a whole.

Something of the same thinking went into the planning of this book. We were tempted to give many more details about each religion. There are many other religions we might have included. Instead, we have spoken of only the great world religions—and even those have been given only a few pages.

Obviously a great deal of valuable information had to be omitted. But by keeping our distance, by not looking for too many details, we have tried to make it possible for you to see the whole picture—the most important things that make one religion different from another.

Sorting Out

Despite all their differences, religions can be arranged according to just a few categories:

A. **One God or many gods?** Does the world have one set of rules, or many?

B. **Optimistic or pessimistic?** Is the world a good place to be made better, or an evil place from which to escape?

C. **Action or belief?** Are people judged by what they do, or by what they think? Are people encouraged to think for themselves, or are they told exactly what is right for them to believe?

D. **Tolerant or intolerant?** Are other beliefs respected, or are good people of other religions viewed as lost souls?

E. **Equal or unequal?** Are people regarded as equals, or are they divided by race, caste, or special powers?

At a tribal gathering in Indonesia, participants wear ceremonial costumes. Every people on earth has its own forms of worship. In this book, we have concentrated only on the world's major religions, to try to see what makes them similar or different.

Where Judaism Fits In

Looking at these categories, we can see that Judaism does indeed have a very special place in the world:

A. **Judaism teaches belief in one God.** In fact, it was Judaism that brought the idea of one God to the world.

B. **Judaism is optimistic.** It teaches that the world can be good, that its beauties are to be enjoyed, and that our job is to make the world ever more wonderful.

C. **Judaism judges actions.** It teaches the importance of good deeds rather than deciding what people should think. Education has traditionally been a very important part of Jewish life so that Jews can think for themselves.

D. **Judaism is tolerant.** It teaches that good people of every religion deserve respect on earth, just as they will be welcomed in the world-to-come.

E. **Judaism insists that every person**—king or laborer, adult or child—**is equal in the sight of God.** Rabbis, though respected for their learning, are not thought of as being part of a superior caste, or as having supernatural powers.

And we may add another point:

F. **Judaism has held true to these beliefs for 4,000 years.**

No other religion fits that description.

Obviously, this is because other religions do not want to do so. Most of them concentrate on escaping from this world and entering some happier state after death.

But Jews continue to believe that our challenge—to serve God by perfecting God's world—is the greatest opportunity given to any people on earth.

Powerful Ideas

Jews also find that the principles taught by our religion have been especially powerful motor ideas. Because of them:

- Judaism has preserved our people for nearly 40 centuries, even against tyrants who hated the ideals of freedom and equality which we taught.

- Judaism's goals, such as doing away with war and poverty, though certainly not yet achieved, have become the stated goals of most of humanity.

Dressed as Queen Esther, an Israeli girl enjoys the holiday of Purim.

Asking the Four Questions at a Passover seder.

The Menorah has been a symbol of Judaism since ancient times. This one stands outside the building of the Knesset, or parliament, in Israel.

- Judaism has given our people the courage to recreate our homeland after nearly 2,000 years of exile.

- Because Judaism asks us to study and to question, Jews have produced thinkers and creators in numbers far out of proportion to our total numbers.

- All this has been accomplished even though Jews have been a tiny minority of the world's population.

An Important Reminder

Having said this, we must remind ourselves—no Jew can claim that he is special simply because he is a Jew. If we are a chosen people, it is because we have been chosen to improve God's world. Our actions may make us special. Simply being Jewish does not.

And Judaism recognizes that other religions may have their value, as long as they teach people to be good. "The righteous of *all* nations, non-Jews as well as Jews, will have a share in the world-to-come."

Yet our basic question has been answered. Is Judaism special? Definitely, *Yes.* It alone of the world's religions has survived for thousands of years teaching the value of life, of equality, and of freedom.

The eighth night of Ḥanukkah.

And Now . . .

And now?

It is for you to decide how to use that freedom.

We hope you will use it to investigate some of the details we have had to leave out of this book. The religions of the world are fascinating to study.

And the wonderful things you can learn about Judaism, and Jewish history, are unlimited.

But then, remember that even as you acquire knowledge, Judaism asks you to do something with it. Our Talmud quotes a rabbi who, nearly 2,000 years ago, taught:

If a person's works exceed his wisdom, that wisdom will still last. But if wisdom is greater than good works, that wisdom will not last. [*Pirke Avot 3:22*]

And what should be the nature of those good works? The answer is in our Bible, and was given to us more than 2,500 years ago:

Let justice well up as waters,
And righteousness as a mighty stream.
[*Amos 5:24*]

APPENDIX

ESTIMATED POPULATIONS OF THE MAJOR WORLD RELIGIONS

Total Christian		1,061,711,600
Roman Catholic	628,990,900	
Protestant	373,769,600	
Eastern Orthodox	58,951,100	
Muslim		554,700,200
Hindu		463,815,200
Buddhist		247,587,500
Confucian		150,984,000
Shinto		32,048,000
Taoist		20,056,000
Jewish		16,932,000
TOTALS		2,547,834,500
TOTAL WORLD POPULATION		4,842,048,000

Source: *1986 Encyclopaedia Britannica Book of the Year*

ESTIMATED RELIGIOUS POPULATIONS OF THE UNITED STATES

Total Protestant		74,210,000
Baptist	25,760,000	
Methodist	12,808,500	
Lutheran	8,477,750	
Presbyterian	3,092,000	
Episcopalian	2,775,500	
United Church of Christ		
(Congregationalist)	1,696,000	
Roman Catholic		52,286,000
Total Jewish		5,835,000
Conservative	2,057,000	
Reform	1,750,500	
Orthodox	525,000	
Reconstructionist	87,000	
Eastern Orthodox		4,052,000
Mormon		3,794,500

Sources: All figures, except those for Jews, are from *1986 Yearbook of American and Canadian Churches*. They represent estimated membership of the various religious groups. The estimated total Jewish population is from the *American Jewish Year Book 1986*. The estimations for the four Jewish movements have been supplied by the North American Jewish Data Bank in New York City, and are based on a combination of nine local surveys representing 1.5 million Jewish households in the United States. These four figures do *not* indicate synagogue membership, but personal responses of people when asked to state their movement identification.

INDEX

Smith, Joseph, 111
Stonehenge, *16*
Sukkot, *31*, *32*
Sunni Muslims, 85
Synagogue, the, 23
Syrian Greeks, *32*

Talmud, 3, 44, 45
Taoism, 72
Temple, Israel's, *78*, 82
Ten Commandments, 22
Thanksgiving, *31*
Tomb, empty (referring to that of Jesus Christ in New Testament narration), 115
Torah scroll, *40*, 41

Torah, the, 2, 4, 22, 23, 24, *33*, 34, 36, 41, 44, 45, 95
Touro Synagogue (Newport, Rhode Island), *42*
Trinity, *94*
Tyndale, William, 106
Tzedakah (righteousness), 36

Unitarians, 108
United States, 6
Universal priesthood of all believers, the doctrine of Protestantism, 103
Universe, 14

Van Eyck, Jan, *90*

Vatican City, 97
Virgin birth, 95, *112*
Virgin Mary, *112*

Williams, Roger, 105
World War II, 6, 9
Women ordained as rabbis, *43*
Worship, 23

Yayoi, annual April Shinto festival in city of Nikko, *76*
Yemenite Jews, *33*
Yom Kippur, *31*
Young, Brigham, *111*

Zen Buddhism, *65*

CREDITS

1 (right) UPI Bettmann Newsphotos; (left) National Archives; 5 NASA; 6 Richard Lobell; 7 Japan National Tourist Organization (JNTO); 9 Robert L. Kern; 10 American Museum of Natural History; 11 (top) American Museum of Natural History; (bottom) Egyptian Government Tourist Office; 12 (left) The Metropolitan Museum of Art; (right) Lee Boltin Picture Library; 13 The Bettmann Archive, Inc.; 14 American Museum of Natural History; 15 (top) Egyptian Government Tourist Office; (bottom) Guatemala Consulate General; 16 (top) British Tourist Authority; (bottom) The Metropolitan Museum of Art, Munsey Bequest; 17 (bottom) Greek National Tourist Organization; 20 Hanna Schreiber, Photo Researchers, Inc.; 22 Religious News Service Photo; 23 Van Bucher, Photo Researchers, Inc.; 24 Consulate General of Israel; 26 Hazel Hankin; 27 (left) Abraham Menashe, Photo Researchers, Inc.; (right) JNTO; 28 Timothy Eagan, Woodfin Camp and Associates; 29 Coalition to Free Soviet Jews; 30 Israel Government Tourism Administration; 31 (bottom) Louis Goldman, Photo Researchers, Inc.; 32 (top) Israel Government Tourism Administration; (bottom left) Scott Weiner, Federation of Allied Jewish Agencies (FAJA), Philadelphia; (bottom right) FAJA; 33 (top) David Harris, Beth Hatefutsoth; 35 (left) Lewis Hine; 37 Egyptian Expedition, The Metropolitan Museum of Art; 38 (top) Religious News Service; 39 Israel Consulate; 40 (left) Israel Office of Information; (right) Norman R. Patz; 42 John Hopf; 43 (top) Virginia F. Stern; (middle) Reconstructionist Rabbinical College; (bottom) Hebrew Union College-Jewish Institute of Religion; 46 Anti-Defamation League; 47 Naomi Patz; 48 Robert L. Kern; 49 (top) Milton Lubarr; (left and bottom) FAJA; 50 (top left) United Jewish Appeal; (top right) Norman R. Patz; (bottom left) Inge Morath, Magnum; (bottom right) FAJA; 52 American Museum of Natural History; 53 Sam Oolie; 54 David A. Wortman; 55 Sam Oolie; 56 Religious News Service; 57 Government of India Tourist Office; 60 Korean National Tourist Office; 61 Ernst Haas; 62 Japan Information Center, Consulate General of Japan; 63 (left) Korean National Tourist Organization; (right) Government of India Tourist Office; 64 Japan Information Center; 65 JNTO; 68 JNTO; 69 T.S. Nagarijan, India Tourism Development Corporation; 70 JNTO; 71 Japan Information Center; 73 Caldwell College; 74 (top) Government of India Tourist Office; (bottom) Darshan Lall, India Tourism Development Corporation; 75 JNTO; 76 JNTO; 78 Israel Government Tourism Administration; 80 UPI/Bettmann Newsphotos; 82 Turkish Culture and Information Office; 83 (left) Norman R. Patz; (right) Turkish Culture and Information Office; 84 Wide World; 86 Victor Laredo, National Tourist Office of Spain; 87 Israel Government Tourism Administration; 88 Israel Government of Tourism Administration; 89 The Israel Department of Antiquities and Museums; 90 The Metropolitan Museum of Art; 92 The Metropolitan Museum of Art; 93 Print by Julius Schnorr von Carolsfeld, Photo Researchers, Inc.; 94 (left) The Metropolitan Museum of Art; (right) Painting by Allessandro Allon, Religious News Service; 95 Art Resource; 96 The Bettmann Archive; 98 (top) Italian Government Travel Office; (bottom) Religious News Service; 99 Ken Wittenberg, Black Star; 100 (top) Laurence E. Keefe, Religious News Service; 100 (bottom) St. Thomas More, Fairfield, N.J.; 101 (top) St. Thomas More; 101 (bottom) Kenneth Garrett, Woodfin Camp and Associates; 102 Religious News Service; 103 The Metropolitan Museum of Art; 105 The Bettmann Archive; 107 Religious News Service; 108 The Bettmann Archive; 109 (top) Israel Government Tourism Administration; (bottom) British Tourist Authority; 111 (top) Israel Government Tourism Administration; (bottom) Church of Jesus Christ of the Latter-Day Saints; 112 (left) Gerard David (central panel). The Metropolitan Museum of Art; (right) Israel Government Tourism Administration; 113 (top) The Metropolitan Museum of Art; (bottom) Wide World; 114 (top) The Bettmann Archive; (bottom) Israel Government Tourism Administration; 115 (top) The Bettmann Archive; (bottom) Sherry Suris; 118 Atlantic Photo; 119 (top) Kenneth Murray, Photo Researchers, Inc.; (bottom) Rainer Kiedrowski, Peter Arnold, Inc.; 120 Religious News Service; 121 Religious News Service; 122 National Archives; 124 Owen-J. Launois from Black Star; 126 (top) Consulate General of Israel; (bottom) FAJA; 127 Jewish Theological Seminary; 130 Religious News Service; 131 Robert L. Kern; 133 Religious News Service; 134 Religious News Service; 136 UPI/Bettmann Newsphotos; 137 Lewis Hine, The Bettmann Archive; 137 Sherry Suris; 140 Joint Distribution Committee; 144 (top) George Holton, Photo Researchers, Inc.; 145 (top) Sherry Suris; (bottom) Stanley K. Patz; 146 Israel Government Tourism Administration; 147 Carol Kitman, Peter Arnold, Inc.